LEADER iD

D1407356

Pearson

At Pearson, we believe in learning – all kinds of learning for all kinds of people. Whether it's at home, in the classroom or in the workplace, learning is the key to improving our life chances.

That's why we're working with leading authors to bring you the latest thinking and best practices, so you can get better at the things that are important to you. You can learn on the page or on the move, and with content that's always crafted to help you understand quickly and apply what you've learned.

If you want to upgrade your personal skills or accelerate your career, become a more effective leader or more powerful communicator, discover new opportunities or simply find more inspiration, we can help you make progress in your work and life.

Every day our work helps learning flourish, and wherever learning flourishes, so do people.

To learn more, please visit us at **www.pearson.com/uk**

The Financial Times

With a worldwide network of highly respected journalists, *The Financial Times* provides global business news, insightful opinion and expert analysis of business, finance and politics. With over 500 journalists reporting from 50 countries worldwide, our in-depth coverage of international news is objectively reported and analysed from an independent, global perspective.

To find out more, visit **www.ft.com**

David Pilbeam
Glenn P Wallis

LEADER iD

DISCOVER YOUR LEADERSHIP PROFILE
LEARN HOW TO IMPROVE!

Harlow, England • London • New York • Boston • San Francisco • Toronto • Sydney
Dubai • Singapore • Hong Kong • Tokyo • Seoul • Taipei • New Delhi
Cape Town • São Paulo • Mexico City • Madrid • Amsterdam • Munich • Paris • Milan

Pearson Education Limited

KAO Two
KAO Park
Harlow CM17 9NA
United Kingdom
Tel: +44 (0)1279 623623
Web: www.pearson.com/uk

First edition published 2018 (print and electronic)

© Pearson Education Limited 2018 (print and electronic)

The rights of David Pilbeam and Glenn P Wallis to be identified as authors of this work have been asserted by them in accordance with the Copyright, Designs and Patents Act 1988.

ISBN: 978-1-292-23263-8 (print)
     978-1-292-23264-5 (PDF)
     978-1-292-23265-2 (ePub)

British Library Cataloguing-in-Publication Data
A catalogue record for the print edition is available from the British Library

Library of Congress Cataloging-in-Publication Data
A catalog record for the print edition is available from the Library of Congress

10 9 8 7 6 5 4 3 2 1
22 21 20 19 18

Cover design by Two Associates
Cover images © Djordje Radivojevic/Shutterstock

Print edition typeset in 9.5/13, Helvetica Neue LT W1G by iEnergizer Aptara® Ltd
Printed by Ashford Colour Press Ltd, Gosport

NOTE THAT ANY PAGE CROSS REFERENCES REFER TO THE PRINT EDITION

CONTENTS

ABOUT THE AUTHORS

David Pilbeam specialises in leadership and performance coaching for individuals and teams. His experience in running businesses and educating leaders enables him to help people to build on their strengths and achieve on-going success. David's style has been described as challenging, motivating and pragmatic. He uses a performance and strengths focussed approach in his work. David is a also coaching supervisor and author.

He has an MA in Coaching and Mentoring Practice, is a Member of the Association for Coaching and the Institute of Coaching, a Master Practitioner in The Leadership Challenge and a Cognitive Processing Profile Accredited Practitioner.

He has 17 years' experience in one-to-one and team coaching, leadership development, coach development and delivering organisational change projects. He has a strong business background having held a number of management roles and worked as an Operations Director in the Leisure Sector. This includes being part of a four person executive team that founded a national business in 1993 and sold for profit in 1999.

He has lived and worked in Asia, Africa and Portugal over a 12 year period and has worked on projects that span across a number of different cultures and nationalities.

Dr Glenn Wallis is Principal at Glenn P Wallis, a boutique coaching consultancy based in London, UK. He is one of the very few people in the world to hold a Doctorate in Coaching and Mentoring. Glenn helps executives and senior leaders develop the introspective skills, advanced thinking and mental resilience required, leading to professional development and enduring outcomes. Glenn is a keynote speaker and author.

As well as his doctorate, Glenn has a Masters in Coaching and Mentoring Practice, is an Associate of the Institute for Coaching, based at Harvard University Medical School, and an active Fellow of the RSA (Royal Society for the encouragement of Arts, Manufactures and Commerce).

Glenn believes passionately in the empirical and professional application of coaching, as distinct from mentoring and other forms of senior leadership support. His work is underpinned by a substantial academic base, as well as nearly 20 years of practical experience working with leaders at all levels within organisations.

Additionally, Glenn's intellectual curiosity and desire to 'democratise coaching' have seen him investigate and develop several methodologies and technology-based tools for virtual coaching.

When not working, Glenn lives with his wife in the London Borough of Richmond upon Thames. He can often be found running along the Thames towpath on Sunday mornings.

INTRODUCTION

Leadership is an intense journey into yourself. You can use your own style to get anything done. It's about being self-aware.

Jeff Immelt, CEO of General Electric

Leader iD is a simple online test you can take as part of this book. It provides a snapshot of you as a leader. It captures your current personal characteristics and leadership skills. Once you know your Leader iD, you are in a very strong position to use it to achieve success for yourself, your team, your boss, your customers and your business. It will help you understand yourself more fully than you do currently and this self-knowledge is a gateway to your development as a great leader.

WHY IS YOUR LEADER iD SO IMPORTANT?

When leaders develop a clear sense of their own identity, their organisation's performance flourishes. Understanding who they are as a person enables them to succeed in the role of 'leader'. Gaining clarity about their sense of self gives them a greater sense of confidence in their own ability to deliver effective leadership and – without fail – they go on to lead well.

Leading well delivers benefits to their colleagues, boss, key stakeholders and customers. It enables their organisation to continue to meet challenges. This is what we want for you.

Less than two-thirds of CEOs in a recent survey felt senior leaders in their organisations were well placed to meet future business challenges. HR directors in the same study felt that only 18% of senior leaders were 'highly capable'. Studies such as these, of which there are many, suggest an oncoming leadership crisis. Well-developed leaders, who are clear and who can flex their approach to suit the challenges they face, will be critical to the future success of any organisation and society.

We have used the principles underpinning Leader iD to coach hundreds of senior leaders who have grown to excel at leading over the last 20 years.

Now you can use them too.

WHY HAVE WE WRITTEN *LEADER iD* NOW?

In our careers as leadership consultants and coaches, we have had the pleasure of working with hundreds of senior leaders and their teams. We have worked with them to achieve goals and challenges and helped many to overcome obstacles and thrive. Yet, particularly recently, we have noticed the relentless pace of organisational change and its direct impacts on many leaders. In the turmoil of day-to-day delivery, leadership gets put on the backburner. Tasks get ticked off on a 'to do list' but real change is seldom well-led and people are rarely developed and challenged as they might be. Many senior leaders do not want to become *very* senior leaders, preferring to remain where they are, for fear of getting overwhelmed by the relentless organisational machine.

In short, many leaders find themselves lost. They don't know what to focus on and they have little sense of themselves as key players in the success of the organisation.

We wanted to take our experiences and share them with you so you can rediscover the clarity you need to become an outstanding leader, even in these most uncertain times.

If you couple this sense of feeling lost with the fact that many organisations are investing less in helping leaders develop – or worse, spending it on outmoded and ineffective development interventions – it is no surprise that CEOs and HR directors have little confidence in their senior leaders to lead. The specialised nature of the work we do means that, whilst we have helped many leaders, we're aware that we could help so many more.

Leader iD is the platform for us to contribute to a much larger leadership community than our direct work allows.

This book is our lifeline to busy, unsettled leaders like you, who are eager to develop and who are convinced they can lead more effectively. We want to help you shape your leadership identity and re-ignite the original motivation you had for signing on the dotted line when someone at some moment in the past said to you: 'We want you to lead.'

WHAT DOES IT TAKE TO BE AN EFFECTIVE LEADER IN TODAY'S WORLD OF WORK?

Today's workplaces are incredible structures. Not only the physical buildings and products and services, but the innovative business models too, adopted across all sectors. Silos and functions are disappearing. Project teams, virtual teams and disparate workers are emerging. Turgid meeting rooms and low-energy sit-downs are being scrapped, whilst standing desks and standing meetings are being introduced. Offices are being dismantled, and pods and open spaces are engineered to replace them. Technology has substituted much human interaction too. Whilst some important things have been lost with the advent of so much technology, when implemented well, it has revolutionised how we work. Agile working, lean methodologies and rapid prototyping are all new approaches to work and innovation.

Each and every one of these changes produces one common effect: increased pace. In today's workplace, speed is all.

It is in this context that leaders have to do their work. Well-equipped leaders will thrive. Leaders that haven't grown and adapted to the new reality will get left further and further behind, even more quickly than their forebears did in the 1980s to 2000s.

Leaders need a new guide on how to lead in this 'new normal'. *Leader iD* is that guide. It provides help and advice on how to 'be' a highly effective leader and how to 'do' highly effective leadership both today and into the future.

For leaders to succeed in this new reality, they will need to be:

- comfortable with ambiguity
- flexible in their thinking
- able to focus on the uniqueness not only of situations but of people
- open to a wide range of diverse views that will challenge the very bedrock of long-held truths, values and beliefs.

The new world of work also requires a new kind of confidence. Such confidence will not come from being a subject expert. It will come from self-awareness and belief in your own abilities to succeed in challenging situations. Leaders particularly need a healthy dose of self-efficacy: they need to believe that their behaviours and actions are responsible for successful outcomes.

Think of it as a kind of faith in yourself. High self-efficacy has positive impacts on the tasks we will undertake, how we undertake them, how long we will endure and how we review our efforts. Leaders with high self-efficacy seek out leadership roles more than those with lower self-efficacy and, all things being equal, they lead more effectively. Importantly, self-efficacy grows with an increasingly clear sense of yourself.

Whilst adapting, flexing and role-modelling, a leader in today's workplace also needs to be developing themselves as well as others. Failure to change personally is not an option. Neither is failure to grow the members of their team, their peers and pretty much anyone else they encounter on a daily basis. Developing others using a well-intentioned cookie-cutter approach is not acceptable either. Leaders need to appreciate the uniqueness of each individual they work with and adapt their style accordingly. This is particularly important with the rapidly changing nature of the workforce.

Millennials will make up 75% of the workforce by 2028. Even if, like us, you don't sign up to the idea of identifying an entire generation born between about 1985 and 2000 with a set of universal drivers, desires and dreams, it is clear that there is a changing expectation around what life and work should be like. If you lead others, you will need to respond to these changing expectations and the high performance standards that will be set for you and your team. To achieve organisational success, the first area of focus for development and growth may well be on yourself.

HOW IS THIS BOOK GOING TO HELP YOU AS A LEADER?

Busy leaders face several challenges when it comes to developing themselves, including the following:

- Organisations are often unwilling to invest in development.
- Development typically is delivered at set times rather than when you need it.
- Organisations typically use a one-size-fits-all approach to developing unique human beings.
- Development programmes often lack the mechanisms for benchmarking where you are now.
- Development programmes even more frequently lack a mechanism for providing evidence of your progress.

Self-awareness is so important for development both from day to day and in the much longer term. Deepening your own self-awareness is crucial for your development but it is also a key ingredient for working with and developing others. The beauty of *Leader iD* is that you will develop your own levels of self-awareness through using our diagnostic tool and working your way through the accompanying chapters.

Once you have completed your Leader iD profile, you can prioritise and tailor your learning. This allows you to maximise the progress you achieve in the most efficient way. Typically, book-based development fails to provide individualised learning. Thankfully, *Leader iD* overcomes that common pitfall by providing you with your own benchmark, a map of how to progress and a rich set of resources for successful improvement.

HOW THE LEADER iD MODEL WORKS AND HOW IT HELPS LEADERS THRIVE

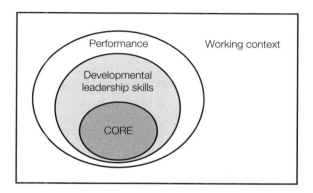

Let's use a familiar metaphor to help explain the Leader iD model: the many-layered and humble onion.

The CORE layer of the Leader iD model represents you. It denotes who you are as a person – your very 'self'. The next layer is the set of skills you display as a leader. The most effective group of these skills for you to master is called 'Developmental leadership skills'. The outer layer represents how the combination of your CORE and developmental leadership skills positively impact 'Performance'. There is no point working on your Leader iD if it fails to improve your own performance, that of your team and of your business.

You, your leadership and the resulting performance don't occur in a vacuum. They happen inside a context. The size and scope of that context depend on innumerable factors. The important thing to remember here is that you are connected to a wider system within which you lead. There is a two-way dynamic relationship between you, your leadership and the context within which you find yourself.

There is another way of interpreting the model: from outside to inside. Typically, we start from the inside and work outwards but it can be helpful, on occasion, to start at the very outside of the model at the 'Working context' and work inwards.

Developing skills and personal traits is hard to do in isolation. Learning is even harder to achieve whilst failing to recognise the context in which leadership is executed. Reflecting on the model from the 'Working context' through 'Performance' and 'Developmental leadership skills' to 'CORE' highlights the impacts of the context in which you lead on each of the other layers of the model. Furthermore, it demonstrates the inter-dependent nature of the elements of a leader's identity.

Keep in mind the performance you need to deliver as a leader, as well as the context you are working within, as we offer you the chance to take your Leader iD diagnostic.

HOW TO READ *LEADER iD*

In Part 1 you will complete your Leader iD profile. Once you have that, you are free to move through the rest of the book as suits your particular situation. More about why you may not want to move through the book from page to page soon, but first let us explain how Parts 2, 3 and 4 pan out.

Part 2 focuses on identity, with a chapter dedicated to each of the elements of identity that we use in our model: compassion, discovery, perspective, determination and balance.

Part 3 focuses on leadership, with a chapter dedicated to each of the developmental excellences we use in our model: embodying excellence, advocating excellence, appreciating excellence and developing excellence.

Part 4 provides you with three tools that will help you to put all you have learnt into practice.

Each chapter within Parts 2 and 3 includes insights. Each insight is aligned to the individual questions set within the Leader iD profiling tool and accompanied by a wealth of tips, exercises and reflections. The intention is for you to draw from the chapters according to your personal Leader iD. You can focus on the areas you need to in the order you want to and you can do so as specifically or as generally as you wish.

Let's briefly look at an example. If, generally, you didn't score well in, let's say, compassion, then read the whole chapter covering compassion and complete all the learning and development activities. On the other hand, if you scored ok in compassion generally, other than in one very specific area, you can go to the specific insight and concentrate on that. The format of the book allows great flexibility in how you shape your development and also enables you to target exactly how you spend your leadership development time.

The insights contained within each chapter have been linked to real-world actions, changes to your thinking, well-tested advice and reflective coaching questions. In our experience, these insights bring about real and lasting change for leaders. Just reading them may produce some differences for you, but real success is possible only if you are willing to take the required steps, every day, to ensure that the development you are looking for is achieved and that the changes you make actually stick.

PART 1

YOUR LEADER
iD PROFILE

CHAPTER 1
THE DIAGNOSTIC TOOL

HOW ARE YOU DOING?

We have dedicated this chapter to presenting our diagnostic tool, the Leader iD profile. It is the outcome of the research upon which we have based this book.

It is a self-assessment tool. It enables you to score how well you think you are doing at each of the nine areas that our research has identified as vital to your development as a leader.

Completing the Leader iD profile is a first step for you to explore the Leader iD model for yourself and to find the best route forward on the journey to future success. It is important to focus fully, dedicating at least an hour of your time to this task. It may not take that long, but be prepared that it might, and remember that it is time well invested, time that will be more than paid back in terms of success in a short period of time.

Completing the Leader iD profile will give you an insight into how you currently shape up against the model and help you to identify priorities that require immediate attention if you are to survive and thrive as a leader, both now and in the future.

Whilst we are all born with a range of abilities, the human characteristics and qualities required to be a leader are open to be developed by anyone. The challenge is knowing what to develop so that your efforts are efficiently spent in improving the right areas. When you look at your Leader iD profile results, you may discover that you are already acting as a leader in some areas. These are strengths for you to build on. The questions at the end of the exercise invite you to reflect on both your areas of strength and weakness, and to make some initial plans for action based on this new awareness.

We encourage you to ask some of your colleagues to evaluate you too. You could also ask them to give you some concrete examples to support their view of the areas in which you excel and the areas where they think you could improve. You can complete the Leader iD profile right here in the book or you can access it online by visiting the following URL: www.glennpwallis.com/leader-id

If you would like to take the 360° feedback version of the Leader iD profile, please go to:

Ready? Let's go ...

YOUR LEADER iD PROFILE

1. The 45 statements in the Leader iD profile describe behaviours that we believe you need to consistently engage in at work in order to achieve future success.

2. The analysis section groups these 45 statements into 9 sets of 5 statements, corresponding to the 9 elements that form the Leader iD model.

3. Work through each of the statements and consider 'How frequently do I engage in the behaviour described?' Then choose the response that best applies to each statement and draw a circle around it.

4. Be honest with yourself and realistic about the extent to which you actually engage in the behaviour. Do not answer in terms of how you would like to behave or how you think you should behave, but how you typically behave on most days, on most projects, with most people.

5. Be thoughtful about your responses. For example, giving yourself all 5s on all items is most likely not an accurate description of your behaviour. Likewise, giving yourself all 1s or 3s may not be an accurate description either. Most people will do some things more or less often than they do other things.

6. If you feel that a statement does not apply to you, it is probably because you don't frequently engage in the behaviour. In that case, assign a rating of 1.

Make sure that you are in a comfortable environment, have all you need (a cup of coffee or your favourite brew perhaps?) and will not be disturbed for at least an hour.

	Never	Rarely	Often	Almost always	Always
1. I invest time and energy in building working relationships with others.	1	2	3	4	5
2. I am kind and generous to others and find time to help people with their challenges.	1	2	3	4	5

	Never	Rarely	Often	Almost always	Always
3. I fit in well to different social situations and put others at ease.	1	2	3	4	5
4. I exercise a sense of duty and social responsibility for the common good of the business.	1	2	3	4	5
5. I focus on helping others to make their best contribution at work.	1	2	3	4	5
6. I am not content with doing something the conventional way if a better way is possible.	1	2	3	4	5
7. I am curious about everything, always asking questions and keen to discover new information.	1	2	3	4	5
8. I consider the available options and evidence before making decisions.	1	2	3	4	5
9. I encourage others to love learning as much as I do.	1	2	3	4	5
10. I provide valuable insight on matters and have a way of looking at the world that makes sense to others.	1	2	3	4	5
11. I am a grateful person who takes the time to express thanks for a job well done.	1	2	3	4	5
12. I am hopeful and encourage others to see a positive future.	1	2	3	4	5
13. I like to laugh and encourage others to see the lighter side where appropriate.	1	2	3	4	5
14. I appreciate the aesthetics of skilled performance in all domains of work.	1	2	3	4	5
15. I express strong and coherent beliefs about the higher purpose and meaning of work.	1	2	3	4	5
16. I do not shrink from threat, challenge or difficulty.	1	2	3	4	5

continued

	Never	Rarely	Often	Almost always	Always
17. I have a clear sense of what is right and wrong and shape my actions accordingly.	1	2	3	4	5
18. I do not get distracted when at work and take satisfaction in completing tasks.	1	2	3	4	5
19. I approach all work with excitement and energy.	1	2	3	4	5
20. I value my own strengths and the strengths of others.	1	2	3	4	5
21. I give people a second chance if they have done something wrong.	1	2	3	4	5
22. I am a careful person who examines all possible choices and consequences before drawing conclusions.	1	2	3	4	5
23. I prefer to let my personal accomplishments speak for themselves.	1	2	3	4	5
24. I am disciplined and in control of my emotions.	1	2	3	4	5
25. I treat people with fairness and dignity.	1	2	3	4	5
26. I set an example by constantly striving to get better and better at what I do.	1	2	3	4	5
27. I deliver on promises and commitments made to others.	1	2	3	4	5
28. I champion organisational values for others.	1	2	3	4	5
29. I act with integrity.	1	2	3	4	5
30. I build a culture of excellence and high performance.	1	2	3	4	5
31. I describe a captivating picture of what the future could look like.	1	2	3	4	5

	Never	Rarely	Often	Almost always	Always
32. I illustrate to others how their ambitions can be fulfilled.	1	2	3	4	5
33. I set high standards for people to live up to.	1	2	3	4	5
34. I speak with clarity and confidence in public forums.	1	2	3	4	5
35. I demonstrate excitement and commitment to the vision.	1	2	3	4	5
36. I make sure that people are rewarded for work that delivers results.	1	2	3	4	5
37. I embrace different perspectives and encourage innovative thinking.	1	2	3	4	5
38. I constantly seek to generate the small improvements in performance that represent progress.	1	2	3	4	5
39. I look outside my team for inspiration and new thinking.	1	2	3	4	5
40. I create an environment in which people feel valued for speaking honestly and are encouraged to share ideas and beliefs.	1	2	3	4	5
41. I build strong relationships through empathy and trust.	1	2	3	4	5
42. I provide and encourage performance-focused feedback.	1	2	3	4	5
43. I treat people as individuals and coach them towards excellence.	1	2	3	4	5
44. I encourage people to exploit their strengths and manage their weaknesses.	1	2	3	4	5
45. I take personal responsibility for helping others raise their performance.	1	2	3	4	5

continued

ANALYSE YOURSELF

Give yourself the same score in points as your answer. That is, if you scored question 1 as a 4, then give yourself 4 points for that question.

Questions 1 to 5

1. _____
2. _____
3. _____
4. _____
5. _____

Total score for COMPASSION:

Questions 6 to 10

6. _____
7. _____
8. _____
9. _____
10. _____

Total score for DISCOVERY:

Questions 11 to 15

11. _____
12. _____
13. _____
14. _____
15. _____

Total score for PERSPECTIVE:

Questions 16 to 20

16. _____
17. _____
18. _____
19. _____
20. _____

Total score for DETERMINATION:

Questions 21 to 25

21. _____
22. _____
23. _____
24. _____
25. _____

Total score for BALANCE:

Questions 26 to 30

26. _____
27 _____
28. _____

29. _____
30. _____
Total score for EMBODIES EXCELLENCE:

Questions 31 to 35
31. _____
32. _____
33. _____
34. _____
35. _____
Total score for ADVOCATES EXCELLENCE:

Questions 36 to 40
36. _____
37. _____
38. _____
39. _____
40. _____
Total score for APPRECIATES EXCELLENCE:

Questions 41 to 45
41. _____
42. _____
43. _____
44. _____
45. _____
Total score for DEVELOPS EXCELLENCE:

Self factors

The first 25 statements describe the mindsets that our research tells us leaders need to practise at work, consistently, in order to build credibility and achieve future success.

COMPASSION   _____ /25
DISCOVERY   _____ /25
PERSPECTIVE   _____ /25
DETERMINATION   _____ /25
BALANCE   _____ /25

Leadership behaviours

The next 20 statements describe the leadership activities that our research tells us that leaders need to engage in at work in order to bring out the best in others and create a culture of excellence.

EMBODIES EXCELLENCE   _____ /25
ADVOCATES EXCELLENCE   _____ /25
APPRECIATES EXCELLENCE   _____ /25
DEVELOPS EXCELLENCE   _____ /25

Total overall Leader iD profile score: /225

INTERPRETING YOUR SCORES

The main purpose of the Leader iD profile is to learn about your relative strengths and weaknesses, so that you can take practical actions based on those insights.

In which self factor did you rate yourself highest? (There may be more than one.)

In which self factor did you rate yourself lowest? (Again, there may be more than one.)

In which leadership behaviour did you rate yourself highest? (Again, there may be more than one.)

In which leadership behaviour did you rate yourself lowest? (Again, there may be more than one.)

What general conclusions can you draw from your scores?

Which areas of your leadership performance are you going to prioritise for improvement?

What are your initial thoughts about how you will go about this?

NEXT STEPS?

Keep your Leader iD profile scores close by as you develop your skills and self-awareness by reading the relevant chapters in this book.

You may want to create your own road map through the book, dipping in and out of the chapters, as your learning from this diagnostic suggests.

CHAPTER 2

DEVELOPING YOU AND YOUR LEADERSHIP

ARE GREAT LEADERS BORN OR MADE?

Great job! You have now completed your Leader iD profile for the first time. You are fully armed with a new and deeper level of self-awareness than you previously had and with that comes power and the catalysts for change. Now we want to share some key thoughts about becoming a leader, what that process involves and how you can ensure you can bring about the sort of development that you want.

In this chapter we'll explore some fundamentals about leadership that may shake the core beliefs you hold about leaders. We'll prompt you to change views about your own capacity to become 'great'. You will get to appreciate your place in the long line of history of great leaders and why it is very possible that you can take a place amongst them. If you are struggling a bit to embrace the idea of your own Leader iD, we can shed some light on why that might be. We'll also encourage you to view your development as a leader as an active, rather than passive, process.

Let's get one thing straight. Being a 'great' leader is not the same as being a 'famous' leader. Many books on leadership hold up examples of well-known leaders who often changed the world. We avoid that approach for two very simple reasons. First, we're not expecting you to change the world: fabulous if you do, but not essential to be considered 'great' in our book. Second, most people we have spoken with understand the possible benefits from reading about Winston Churchill, Joan of Arc, Martin Luther King, Benazir Bhutto, Ghandi and many more, yet struggle to see themselves achieving such heights. The incredible achievements of such leadership greats make them seem inaccessible.

Names such as Steve, Marie, Marc, Ramanjeet and Esther populate our list of great leaders. All 'normal' people doing normal jobs to a very high standard. People who have moved from being outstanding in their chosen fields to being excellent leaders of teams and organisations.

People who typically remain unknown outside their immediate circle and industry but within which are deemed to be great leaders. People very much like you. Being a great leader is fully within your capability.

THE IMPORTANCE OF CONTEXT

Leadership styles often reflect the times and contexts within which they are exercised. The Industrial Revolution largely saw a dictatorial leadership style where what the leader said (the factory owner) was expected to be followed unquestioningly. Employees were a resource. In opposition to this, powerful workers' groups and trade unions sprang up, at which point the best leaders realised there was a shift in power.

We are now living in a more pluralistic society where choices and freedoms for most are virtually limitless. With the advent of technology and rapidly changing workplaces, leadership theory has expanded to reflect this and includes a wide range of approaches to achieving highly effective leadership:

- servant leadership
- authentic leadership
- brave leadership
- integrated leadership.

The main point is this: in order to lead effectively, you need to be finely attuned to the context within which you lead. That is not the same thing as being wholly reactive to the context – especially if it is not conducive to great work – but to lead in opposition to, or denial of, the context would be short-sighted at best and career-limiting at worst.

EVOLUTION: IS BEING A LEADER IN YOUR GENES?

Were you born a natural leader or does nurture play a stronger part than genetics in shaping your ability to lead? This is an age-old question upon which the following paragraphs shed some light.

The genus *Homo*, which includes modern humans, is about 2.5 million years old and, from the earliest days, people lived in small bands of family and extended family. Basic decision making was a critical skill to ensure survival and would have been accompanied by friction and conflict. From within these small groups, certain individuals would have emerged as those who could manage conflict, keep the group together and help shape the decision making that was required to survive.

Furthermore, people would have to be brought together at specific times when a task required more than one person such as hunting or building a shelter. At times like these, leaders would have emerged who were good at drawing a disparate band of individuals into a more efficient group (Bloom, 2000). The individuals that emerged at these key points were the earliest form of leader.

What has the impact been on our genetic code over the last 2.5 million years of some individuals taking these leadership roles? According to some researchers, the role of a leader is deeply embedded in human psychology, as is the concept of follower (van Vugt & Ronay, 2014). Indeed, recent research has identified that there is, in fact, a genetic link to leadership. The results show that leadership is associated with a tiny bit of genetic code, creatively referred to as rs4950 (De Neve, Mikhaylov, Dawes, Christakis & Fowler, 2013). It seems, then, that the latest thinking identifies an element of genetic influence on your ability to lead.

As we have seen, being a highly effective leader is the result of a combination of both nature and nurture. If we were pushed, we would say that the balance is skewed in favour of the work you do on yourself, the skills you learn and the context in which you lead. In other words, in relation to becoming a leader, nurture trumps nature (probably).

MARIE

Marie was, in her own words, 'an ok manager' at a large UK retailer. She didn't view herself as a leader and resisted the idea that she was a very influential part of the organisation she worked for. She thought about herself in this way, despite the fact that her line manager thought she was incredibly good at her job and was leading one of the highest performing teams in the business. Those people she led would have walked over hot coals for her too. However, Marie's internal script was telling her she was better off playing small, not stepping into the limelight that others were trying to shine on her, avoiding the idea of being a senior player in the business. Others recognised her as a leader even though she failed or refused to do so herself. The challenge for Marie was that the business wanted to promote her but would do so only when she developed an identity that was more in line with other senior leaders in the business.

Following some executive coaching sessions, Marie gradually began to acknowledge the positive impacts she was having on people within and beyond the organisation and the incredible results she was able to facilitate. She was provided with feedback from all around the business that told a story of her own high achievement. Slowly, she began to develop her view of her own identity as a leader, from someone at the beck and call of more senior people to a leader in her own right who was able to positively impact the success of the whole business. Marie was recently promoted and, the last time we spoke, she was loving her new responsibilities.

Fortunately for Marie, she worked in an organisation that valued leadership, took time to develop her and clearly wanted her to succeed. The context was all important to her success.

If you find yourself in a similar situation to Marie, could you rely on your organisation to be that supportive of you?

Leadership is not dependent upon your position in your organisation, but is largely a product of your mindset rather than a specific number of people you have responsibility for or the job title you have. You can demonstrate great leadership, whether you were born with a set of leadership capabilities or have to rely on learning them.

The challenges will be partly from the context in which you find yourself leading – the culture within which you do your work and your own motivation and beliefs around the importance of leading well. The good news is that, once you decide that you will commit to becoming a great leader, it is within your gift to achieve it. You can work on your own identity and combine that with developing a skill set. You can start this process right here, right now.

WHAT IS IDENTITY?

Identity is an academic topic that philosophers and psychologists have examined at length for much of history. It is a term that often is interchanged with other related words such as character, personality, individuality and 'the self'. These terms themselves have also generated many thousands of journal articles and hundreds of books. Identity is clearly big business. 'Who am I?' is, after all, a central question to human existence.

For the purposes of Leader iD, identity is defined as:

> *How you are perceived by yourselves and by others. It is not just about how you look (your external identity). It is about how you feel (your internal identity).*

DEFINING LEADERSHIP

The second term we need to define for the purposes of this book is leadership and what it is to be a leader. We knew there was a lot of literature on identity but it pales into insignificance when compared to the work on leadership. Leadership is clearly very big business, with over $14bn spent on leadership development in the USA alone every single year.

It will be a relief for you to know that we have a simple way to define leadership within organisations for the purposes of this book too:

You are a leader if you enable positive organisational performance and behaviours in human beings, including yourself.

We don't waste time distinguishing between manager and leader. You manage tasks, projects and deadlines. You lead people to perform. We're also not concerned about *where* you are in the organisation or the title you hold. Being a leader isn't about your title. It is about the way you are and what you do. Indeed, our definition allows for the fact – no, insists upon the fact – that as a *minimum* you need to be enabling *yourself* to perform positively within your organisation, in order to qualify as a leader.

WHAT KIND OF LEADER DO YOU WANT TO BE?

In the next few pages we will ask you to consider your leadership philosophy and the fundamentals of leadership development. We will share our developmental model for leadership, which you can use to guide you on your journey towards discovering and implementing your own Leader iD.

WHAT IS YOUR PHILOSOPHY OF LEADERSHIP?

This is the question Nelson Mandela (played by Morgan Freeman) asks Francois Pienaar (Matt Damon), captain of the South Africa rugby team, during a superb scene in the film *Invictus*, the story of the 1995 Rugby World Cup in South Africa.

Highly developed leaders appear to be able to articulate a clear personal philosophy of leadership. This may be influenced by their past experiences, or cultural, political or psychological factors. Developing a coherent and acceptable story of how you want to lead is an essential step if you are to lead with confidence. Your philosophy of leadership exists within you but may still need to be discovered. Developing and growing Leader iD means identifying the leadership qualities that you have that others will be drawn to follow and beginning to use and develop them consciously.

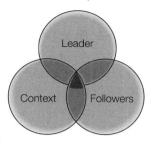

The figure above shows how developing great leadership requires attention in all three elements: the leader, their followers and a context within which to lead.

Leadership is a process of social interaction, both with followers and in the organisational context. Therefore, development takes place at the intersection of these three elements, as illustrated above. No single element alone can provide the stimulus for leadership growth (or delivery of results).

This figure shows developed leadership capability as the leader increases their relationship between themself and their followers and the context.

Quiet reflection is useful for development only when there is action to reflect upon. Action without reflection ensures that learning occurs only sub-consciously, if at all. Ignoring the context you are leading in suggests a one-size-fits-all approach based on the assumption that you can translate what worked elsewhere into a new environment and 'press go'. Only by paying attention to all three domains can you ensure that learning takes place and that an appropriate Leader iD be constructed that – based on your core 'self' – will deliver results.

Leadership and me

Now answer some questions to warm you up to the task of developing your own leadership philosophy and set you on the road to discovering your Leader iD.

continued

1. Who are the leaders you admire? Pick two or three leaders you admire and consider the following:

   - What was it that they achieved?

   - What did they actually do to achieve this success? How did they go about it?

   - What leadership qualities did they exhibit that meant that others chose to follow them?

   - What can you take from your answers here that will help you get clarity around the leader that you want be?

2. How well do I know the context I am leading in? Consider the following:

   - What are the market challenges facing the business?

   - What are the expectations of me from my key stakeholders?

   - What is the business strategy and my team's expected contribution?

   - Who is in my team and what are their strengths, weaknesses, values and challenges?

   - What results am I expected to deliver?

3. How well do you know yourself and the leader you want to be? Take a few minutes to consider the kind of leader you want to be:

   - What do I want my followers thinking, feeling and saying about their experience of being led by me?

   - What do I want the impact of my leadership to be?

   - What would my reputation as a leader need to be in order for me to increase my chances of being successful with my current or future team?

   - What leadership qualities do I need to exhibit in order to create followers in this context?

Answering these questions is not easy, is it? Neither is developing and growing your Leader iD. We know from experience and research that leadership is a visible pattern of behaviours and thought processes that can be learned by anyone. However, not everyone wants to or is ready to do the work necessary. What does getting to work look like then? Let's explore.

HOW DOES LEADER iD DEVELOP?

Understanding self and the leader you want to be is vital if you are to develop a leadership style that reflects your personal beliefs and values. A greater awareness of 'self' leads to deeper understanding of how you affect your followers through how you show up and what you do. It also has a dramatic effect on work contexts – excellent leaders are not only able to navigate the work environment effectively but can also shape it. Excellent leaders create great places to work.

Critically in our model, the 'self' is seen as an instrument of leadership. Understanding the self, looking after it and checking in on its quality is core to becoming the leader you want to be.

The primary instrument of leadership is the self – in this case you. The tools of leadership all exist within you. Developing Leader iD requires mastery of 'you'. It is not about developing new techniques. Rather, it is about leading from a position of knowing who you are. The development of traditional leadership skills is interwoven with your developing self as leader – they are mutually reinforcing. In essence, this can be a career-long process but speeded up with focus on self-development.

The outcome of any event or activity is profoundly affected by who we show up as and that is determined largely by our identity or who we believe our self to be.

SAMI

Sami had a propensity to say things when under pressure in meetings that he would regret later – in fact, often he would hate himself for it. Sometimes, he would pass it off as not 'suffering fools gladly'. The outcome of those meetings, even though he had all the necessary technical skills, was that nothing got done – people were afraid to speak up and share their real views and feelings.

Sami grew frustrated with this and, after seeking help, began to take more notice of his behaviour and the effect he was having. With support, he resolved to change how he 'showed up' by consciously paying attention to how well he listened and learned from others and, through open dialogue with his team, he developed fresh perspectives.

Preserving the essence of who Sami believed he was and adapting his leadership to the context and particular needs of followers was central to his transformation.

THE FUNDAMENTAL PRINCIPLES

Excellence is not the result of some mysterious quality that exists inside us or inspirational thoughts. Rather, it is the outcome of a routine or some habitual processes. It requires work, motivation and attention to what we call the fundamental principles.

LEARNING AND DEVELOPMENT

Learning and development often are used interchangeably in organisations to describe the work of the department that bears this name. However, there is a growing body of research that suggests that, whilst there is a strong connection between the two, there is also an important distinction.

Learning, in terms of growing your Leader iD, relates to a process of discovering new ways of doing things. Often, this is stimulated by the need to solve new problems or test out new approaches, such as those recommended in this book. This learning typically leads to adding more knowledge, skills and competencies.

When we talk about 'development' we really mean growing the capacity to adapt to increasingly complex environments in a way that is sustainable.

We all have the potential to develop throughout life – just as we are able to change physically, we are able to change and adapt the way we view and respond to the environment in which we find ourselves. A more highly developed leader is, typically, able to think with greater clarity where there are increasing levels of complexity and uncertainty. Whilst research suggests that less than 1% of us have the potential to operate at the very highest levels of development consistently, we all have the capability to develop, to some extent, under the right conditions. We may do this in the following situations:

- Where we encounter new, complex and disruptive experiences that require us to break out of traditional work habits in order to succeed.
- When we are exposed to people with different views of the world, whether cultural, through training or from a different background.
- Through the integration of new perspectives brought about by learning through experience.

THINKING ABOUT DOING IS NOT DOING!

Intentions and plans, no matter how noble, are not action. Your Leader iD will develop through a combination of thought and action – practice. That is to say, whilst there is a direct link between volume of practice to learning and progress, what appears to matter even more is what this practice consists of. In order to develop your leadership capacity, you will be required to see practice as an opportunity to stretch and test yourself. Practising the right things, with a high degree of frequency and intensity, leads to improved leadership performance.

So, developing your Leader iD requires you to allocate significant amounts of time to practise but also to be clear on:

- what specifically you should be practising
- how specifically you should be practising it
- the specific skills, or other abilities, that you need to acquire.

The best leaders are learners who understand the importance of focused practice and implement it to fulfil their potential, often appearing to be achieving step-change improvements continuously. However, when you talk with them you begin to realise that this is an illusion. Development rarely comes in giant leaps. Growth occurs through a high number of small improvements that, over time, add up to something big. They are making the best possible choices about where to focus their attention in order to get the best possible return for their effort.

CHOICE AND CHANGE

By reading this book you are taking control of your own development – we want to encourage this as it is critical. People develop as leaders fastest when they feel responsible for their own progress, rather than waiting for HR, their manager, trainer or coach to prompt them. We want you to jump out of the passenger seat and into the driver's seat of your own development.

A strong leader is fixated with ensuring that their talent is developed to the maximum extent possible. They see it as their own responsibility to make the most of who they are. You will be an excellent leader or an average one based on the choices you make – not the choices of others.

WAKING UP AND GROWING UP

Waking up in leadership terms means setting aside any desire for controlling others and opening yourself up to the possibility that your version of reality may be only one interpretation. Effective leaders are open to fresh perspectives and become much more flexible in their approach. They are open to learning and place a high value on relationships with others. The quality of their thinking and problem solving increases. Their ability to see the broader impact of their work and its higher meaning is enhanced.

For many leaders we talk to, the process of waking up and beginning to grow up begins with stepping out of who you think you are and allowing yourself to explore and experience who else you might be – the leader you want to be. Others describe waking up as the realisation that they can choose to look at those who they lead through different channels (or lenses):

■ **Channel one:** where you see physical bodies in front of you that are all different but distinguishable only by their physical characteristics, such as tall, slim, good looking, handsome, balding, well dressed, etc.

■ **Channel two:** where you see people's roles, performance, contribution and the 'human resource'.

■ **Channel three:** where what you see when you look at others is a whole human being (just like you) looking back at you. You notice their strengths, hopes, dreams and emotions and can begin to make real connections with them.

You can develop the ability to change channels at will and that requires you to notice which channel you are on first. This sounds easy but it takes practice, particularly in the heat of everyday working life.

> What do you see when you look at the people in your team? Are they warm-blooded breathing bodies that just happened to show up at work or are they people who have come to work with the intention of giving their best (just like you)?

LOOKING IN AND LOOKING OUT

Herminia Ibarra, Professor of Leadership at INSEAD, has spent several years studying how people come to define themselves as leaders. She suggests that they do this through doing the work of leadership, which stimulates an internal and an external process – one effecting the other. By doing leadership work they build their reputation and credibility, which in itself can change how they see themselves.

We can advance our own depth as leaders by looking inside and understanding our nature, drives, motivation, thought patterns and intuitions – and looking out by engaging with others, new concepts and ideologies, in order to generate fresh insights that will add meaning to our work with followers. How we show up in the rational objective world is built on our internal world – energy, feelings and thoughts – and often these are fuelled by our experience and the way we process these experiences.

Exceptional leaders systematically seek to understand and develop every factor that contributes to achieving their goals. They acquire knowledge and, more importantly, take action based on that knowledge to ensure that increased understanding is put to maximum use. This learning 'in the thick of it' results from a structured and disciplined approach to reviewing progress regularly in order to establish lessons learned. They ask themselves questions at the end of every day, or after key events, such as:

- What was my intended outcome?
- What was my actual outcome?
- What behaviours of mine contributed to this outcome?
- What new things did I learn about 'how' and 'where' I/we may need to focus in the future?
- What did I reinforce that I already knew?
- What do I still need to find out?
- What do I want to sustain or improve for next time?

It is an illusion that the best leaders are constantly on the run – bouncing from one meeting to another, one call to the next, constantly responding to emails. They are all highly productive individuals that don't lack energy, but they place a high value on making time for reflecting on what is working, what isn't and how they can get better. And then they create the time and space for others to do the same.

BEING A LEADER AND DOING LEADERSHIP

Being a leader refers to demonstrating the personal qualities associated with leadership strength, such as compassion, determination and learning. Doing leadership is concerned with evoking excellence in others through describing success vividly, developing it in others through coaching and showing appreciation for excellent performance. Being is about possessing the qualities of a leader and doing is the practice of leadership.

Developing your Leader iD requires that you pay attention to both and in doing so grow the capability to adapt and get results in multiple contexts and social situations. Our Leader iD diagnostic provides you with the opportunity to consider both sides of this equation and the relationship between the two.

A DEVELOPMENTAL MODEL

Our developmental model shows the developmental process for Leader iD. It is supported by the fundamental principles outlined above and acts as a navigation aid to help you work with this book from this point forward. You do not need to be a slave to it to develop effectively. We are inviting you to consider all four corners of the model in your own way, not necessarily to move through them in sequence.

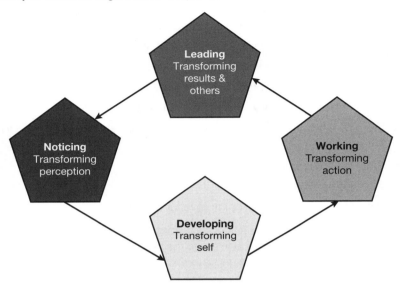

NOTICING

It is often the case that the awareness resulting from paying attention to what is happening to you, to those around you when you are in their presence and the environment in which you are operating, provides the catalyst for change. This is the basis upon which you choose to try some new approaches. Noticing when things need to change can result from internal recognition or from external sources, such as feedback.

Pay attention to what is happening around you and you will quickly get a sense of what needs to be done. Your priorities emerge from these needs when considered alongside the context you are leading in and the goals of the business. Learning to step back to witness what is happening and observing yourself in action is key here. 'Ah, isn't that interesting' is a more useful reflection rather than simply reacting to what is happening in front of you.

By completing our Leader iD diagnostic in the next chapter you will also develop greater awareness of your leadership strengths and weaknesses. From there you will be encouraged to prioritise and pay attention to some specific thought processes and behaviours that will set you on your way to developing your Leader iD.

DEVELOPING

Developing a leader's self can follow on effectively only from 'noticing'. This work is undertaken individually as you explore your values and sense of purpose and their impact on how you lead and how you want to show up as a leader. A developing leader will notice how they go about their business day to day – what is working and what isn't – and experiment in order to discover new and more effective ways to achieve higher levels of leadership performance and a greater understanding of self.

This work is also focused on exploring five key areas of self in relation to Leader iD. In our model and throughout this book we are inviting you to pay attention to the following in particular:

- determination
- perspective
- balance
- discovery
- compassion.

In this phase of the model you are waking up to new possibilities. You become aware that there is a different way of making sense of the world and that doing things in a new way is possible. The Leader iD diagnostic opens up this area for you and provides the insight necessary for you to prioritise your self-development.

WORKING

Working is the externalising phase of the internal work undertaken in the 'developing' phase. Greater mindfulness and reflection help leaders act and review in order to make continuous improvement to their leadership.

This is where we invite you to get to work on the external practices of leadership that form our model. How are you going to:

- embody
- advocate
- appreciate
- develop

in your context and do so in ways that are consistent with your developing sense of the leader you want to be? Parts 2 and 3 will provide you with insights to help you get started. It will ensure that your assumptions about leadership are analysed and challenged. It will encourage you to develop new assumptions and test them out as being new possibilities for your Leader iD.

LEADING

Learning about yourself and about leadership are not the same as leading. Leaders extend their work beyond themselves to generate excellence in organisational results and in those they lead. Leading is about doing – doing something every day to learn something more about leading.

This is about experimentation with different leadership selves and discovering the leader you want to be, gauging the impact you have on others and the work they do. Ultimately, this is about deliberate practice and acting on the work done in the previous three phases of the model.

Leadership ID develops after considerable practice and effort in the field, when new ideas about what works get stronger and start to dominate the previous views. A new level of leadership approach starts to make more sense than the old one.

A NOTE ON THE STRUCTURE OF THE INSIGHTS

The following 9 chapters, from 3 to 11 inclusive, represent the elements of the Leader iD model and the diagnostic you have already completed. Each chapter contains five insights relating directly to a question in the diagnostic. They will help you to identify where you want to read and learn, quickly and easily.

In Part 2, Chapters 3 to 7 use a familiar framework for presenting you with strategies, tips and practical advice for developing yourself as a leader:

- **Believe:** your beliefs around a particular area will impact – positively or negatively – how you respond as a leader.

- **Think:** your beliefs underpin your thinking, so there is no surprise perhaps that, if you change your beliefs, you can change your thinking. But, you can also begin to change your beliefs by adopting new ways to think about situations.

- **Say:** sometimes a little help to enable us to engage our brain before we open our mouth can be invaluable advice, so we have given you some hints and tips on how to phrase your comments and thoughts. Initially, this might feel a bit awkward, until you have practised them sufficiently for them to become more natural.

■ **Do now:** we are great believers in the joint power of reflection and action. Neither is as powerful alone as when leaders combine the two. So, we have provided practical tips for you to try out here and now.

■ **Ask yourself:** before, during and after you have experimented with new thinking and new ways of doing things, we have finished each insight with a set of questions that, if we had been coaching you in person, we might well have asked you.

In Part 3, Chapters 8 to 11 use a slightly different framework to emphasise the practical nature of leadership:

■ **Leading my team:** this section encourages you to take practical action with the team you lead. You don't have to take every single action at the same time, but select the advice you think best fits what you need to achieve.

■ **Leading my organisation:** whether you lead the whole organisation or a part of it, you are a leadership resource for the whole. You have a responsibility to set a standard and lead, wherever you are required to do so. This section directs your attention to action within this wider leadership arena.

PART 2

CORE INSIGHTS RELATING TO IDENTITY

CHAPTER 3
COMPASSION

AN INTRODUCTION TO COMPASSION

Leaders who have a clear sense of their own identity place a high value on their professional relationships with others and, in particular, with those whose goals they share. They are generous to others and are never too busy to help colleagues with their challenges. Effective leaders are aware of the motives and feelings of other people. They know what to do to fit in to different social situations and how to put others at ease. They exercise a sense of duty and social responsibility for the good of the business and are humble about their achievements, preferring to let others take the credit for success.

RELATIONSHIPS

1. Invest time and energy in building working relationships with others. Or put another way: relationships are at the heart of effective leadership.

WHY ARE RELATIONSHIPS SO IMPORTANT?

It is important that you appreciate just how central the building of relationships is to effective leadership and understand its positive impact on trust, understanding, mutual respect and support. These things in turn are vital for your own psychological well-being, physical health and high performance – as well as those you lead.

Capable leaders know that having a small number of significant relationships contributes to improved leadership performance. Those key relationships can be found within your organisation and beyond. Indeed, leaders recognise that we never deliver success alone, and that 'supporters' are vital to success. There are always others involved in bringing about our victories, which by extension make them part of a shared triumph.

Pressure does strange things to relationships. In the face of high demands, the temptation is to retreat to your office and hunker down, determined to resolve a crisis alone and demonstrate independence of thought. However, this is precisely the time when you should be reaching out to others. The best leaders are aware of this tendency to isolate themselves when under stress. It's at this point they reach out to their support networks.

We don't want you to think that such relationships are developed purely for the benefit of the leader. *No!* Develop relationships for mutual benefit. Make time for meeting people with the objective of discussing how you can help *each other* to do better at work, and share knowledge and check understanding of what the business or team is trying to achieve. Investing time in these conversations in a considered and systematic way saves a great deal of time and emotional energy, especially when the going gets really tough.

So, what can you do to develop strong relationships with others? You can believe, think, say, do and reflect.

BELIEVE

The best leaders we have worked with hold two core beliefs about the importance of building deep, mutually beneficial working relationships:

- The leader is there for the benefit of each of their team members, not the other way around.
- Deep, positive relationships can be an end in themselves. Strong leaders don't look primarily for what they can get out of such connections. They invest time in others because they know the more you put in, the more you can get out.

THINK

Thought patterns mirror your beliefs. Successful leaders tend to think often about how they are impacting business relationships that they have or want to have. Leaders are aware that a call to someone they have not contacted for a while is time well invested. When in conversation they will be thinking about how they are presenting themselves, what the impacts could be on the relationship and the business, and they adjust their approaches accordingly.

SAY

One way to ensure that meaningful relationships are built on trust is for leaders to use 'I' in conversations less and 'you' and 'we' more. Such a linguistic switch changes where the focus falls in a conversation – away from the leader towards the other person. It develops a sense of being genuinely valued by the leader. A word of caution: this often proves to be a simple but not easy change to make.

DO

Professional service firm guru David Maister has offered leaders some great advice for developing high trust relationships really quickly through focusing on four important elements, summarised below.

- **Be credible:** consider the words you use as a leader, the experience and skills you bring and the ways in which people experience you. For example, 'Report back to me at the end of every day with your progress' indicates low trust, whereas 'I look forward to seeing it when it is done. Any questions or obstacles along the way that need my help, don't hesitate to ask' indicates high trust.

- **Be reliable:** ensure that your intentions are always followed through with action. The certainty of your behaviour provides a sanctuary for people to do great work.

- **Be open:** encourage people to share confidential information by listening and demonstrating empathy in your response.

- **Be 'other-oriented', not self-focused:** the more your people, co-workers, direct reports and partners sense you are genuinely interested in helping them to explore how good they can be, the more trust builds.

Do these four things consistently and you will develop effective relation-ships built upon high levels of trust. The following exercise will also help.

REFLECT

1. Which colleagues would I turn to in challenging times? Make a list.
2. How do I rate the strength of each relationship out of 10, with 10 being high?
3. For each person, ask:

- Why have I given that rating to each person?
- Which of these relationships needs more work?
- What sort of investment does each relationship need?
- How will I build trust and mutual respect with each person? Hint: remember the four behaviours above.
- How will I sustain the relationship over time?

GENEROSITY

2. I am kind and generous to others and find time to help people with their challenges. Or put another way: it's now your job to help others succeed.

We need leaders to be credible. They need to know what they are talking about and to have a personal track record of success. Becoming a high-performing leader requires that you step beyond this expectation and make it a priority to show compassions through supporting the development and performance of others. Their success, after all, is your success.

Helping others succeed requires placing yourself in their service, a concept first brought to the attention of the business world by Robert Greenleaf in his exceptional work on *Servant Leadership*. Greenleaf says:

> *A servant-leader focuses primarily on the growth and well-being of people and the communities to which they belong.*

To do this, leaders make themselves available and make time for others. They focus on building confidence in others, rather than undermining it, and on developing expertise in others, rather than demonstrating their own expertise.

This requires a genuinely generous mindset. Faking generosity in order to achieve some other more self-serving end will not work. People will see through it.

Sounds a bit too good to be true? A bit soft and fluffy? Still not convinced? Let's throw some academic evidence at it then.

In *Give and Take*, Adam Grant, Professor of Management at the Wharton School of Business at the University of Pennsylvania, argues that one quality that determines how successful a person becomes is how well they share their time, resources and knowledge. A person's reputation for unselfishness wins them admiration and loyalty, even though they do not seek it. This enables them to create stable relationships that ultimately permit them to deliver significant results.

So, what can you do to cultivate a generous attitude? You can believe, think, say, do and ask yourself...

BELIEVE

If you hold any doubts about the importance of generosity, try reflecting on beliefs you hold in relation to helping others.

GLENN

Glenn used to believe that you had to make your own way in life. He saw life as a competition: you survived and thrived through your own efforts. Not a great mindset from which to demonstrate generosity to others. His beliefs originated from a range of influences: parents, teachers, lecturers and sports coaches.

Through questioning his own beliefs, Glenn came to recognise how the generosity of others had helped him to succeed. He now spends much of his working and private life helping others.

THINK

A great way to develop your generous spirit when working with other people is to ask constantly how you can add value to them. Rather than spending your time in your own head thinking about what you can get out of a conversation or a relationship, consider how you might make the other person's life a little easier, a bit fuller or more rewarding. Set out to be helpful from the get-go.

SAY

'How can I help you with that?' Simple! It's no more complicated than just seeking to help. Well, actually it's not quite that simple.

We have words of warning: don't overuse this phrase, especially resist employing it when you could just look around and suggest what you could do to help. Leaders who take the time to think about how they can help are a blessing. The following exercise will help you to be one of these leaders.

DO

Here are five steps you can take to become more generous.

1. Write the names of the three most generous people you know.
2. Identify three ways in which each person is generous.
3. Note any ideas your examples provide about how you could be more generous towards those who look to you for leadership.
4. List the potential benefits to you and your team of you being more generous.
5. If you are not going to be generous and make time to develop others, what are you spending your time doing? Don't like the answer? Then change.

ASK YOURSELF

1. Which three people I know are facing significant challenges, either at work or in their personal life, at the moment?

2. What specifically is challenging about the situation each of these people face?

3. How can I help make each of their situations a little (or a lot) better? Refer to your notes from the exercise above to help. You'll need to be sensitive to the sort of person that they are and what you know of how they might prefer you to offer help (remember Glenn's story about not being easy to help).

4. What steps do I need to take first with each person so that I can help them master the challenges that they face?

5. How am I going to ensure I commit to these first steps? What timelines are practical?

PUT OTHERS AT EASE

3. I fit in well to different social situations and put others at ease. Or put another way: wow! How do they make it look so effortless?

Are you the kind of leader who people back away from when you walk into a room or one towards whom people gravitate? Do you put people on edge because they are worried about what you might say to them or do people flourish in your company and express themselves fully, knowing it is safe to do so?

We know a number of leaders who run the risk of isolating themselves from others. In doing so, they reduce the reach of their influence to no further than those who are, for whatever reasons, willing to respect the title 'leader' – even if they cannot respect the person.

Such leaders pride themselves on their scariness. Guess what? People go out of their way to avoid them and keep their company only when they have to. Often, such leaders are blissfully unaware this is happening. People are too afraid to tell them about the impact they are having and think that the leader probably would receive the feedback as positive in any case. Worse, direct reports are required to spend time and energy figuring out the best way to work with these people, second-guess their mood, pick their moment, not ask the difficult questions or dare to present an alternative view.

Do you know leaders like this?

The price you pay for failing to put people at ease in your company is that people will:

■ fulfil the basic requirements of their job description and no more (if you are lucky)

■ ensure that you never hear the full story and will withhold truths about failures

■ never come close to trusting you – the foundation of team performance

■ relegate your requests and pay scant attention to your direction and advice

■ gossip about you, some of which may be true and quite a lot that won't be.

So, what can you change in order to be one of those leaders that people look at and think 'How do they make it look so effortless?' You can believe, think, say, do and ask yourself.

BELIEVE

If you hold any of these six self-limiting beliefs, you need to change your internal dialogue as these beliefs do not help you to show up as a leader:

■ I'm an introvert and this stuff doesn't come easily to me.

■ I'm not a people person.

■ I don't have presence like others do.

■ I can't change who I am.

■ Others are reaching out, so why should I?

■ I have built a reputation for being tough and it has served me well to this point.

Changing your internal dialogue and hence your self-limiting beliefs may not be easy but it is necessary for you to be effective. Doing so requires thinking, saying and doing things differently.

THINK

First, acknowledge that things won't change if you consider being at ease with others is either not for you or not sufficiently important. If you do want to transform, then start by accepting its importance and committing to change. One of the simplest changes you can make to your thinking is to get out of your own head. Focus on thinking about others and not over-focusing on the thoughts and feelings you are having. Preventing such over-analysis is a great place to start.

SAY

In our work as leadership coaches, we regularly witness that the leaders who are most confident around others, though not reluctant to speak about themselves, prefer to spend time learning about, understanding and appreciating what is important to others. They remove their egos by focusing conversation on those around them. You too can focus attention and conversation on those around you. It is a very liberating approach to 'getting out of your own head'.

DO

Here are five simple steps you can do right now to start the process of being more confident around others:

1. Put down the phone, switch off email and get out from behind your desk. Speak to people about what they are working on. Offer help and support.

2. Be there for people. Practise the art of purposeful wandering. It may feel uncomfortable initially and people may be unsettled by it. But make it a habit and notice the impact on you and others.

3. Find some people outside your direct team. Explore what is happening in their part of the business. Invest a chunk of time with them and get into the detail.

4. Have lunch in the canteen – you will, no doubt, freak out a few people in the beginning but, if you are open, genuine and consistent, eventually people will sit next to you, rather than exit for the local sandwich bar.

5. At events, get around the room, shake some hands and look people in the eye (but not for too long).

ASK YOURSELF

1. What are the reasons that stop me from being at ease around others?

2. What's really going on here?

3. To what extent do I believe I can change the way I operate?

4. What small step will I commit to do today to start the process?
5. Reflecting on this first step, ask what went well, what were the responses of others and of myself and what will I do next?

DUTY

4. I exercise a sense of duty and social responsibility for the common good of the business. Or put another way: doing the right thing is always the right thing to do.

Accomplished leaders think and act beyond their own self-interest. They work for the good of the team or the business and feel a strong sense of duty. They want to work for the progress of society and have strong orientation to help others succeed. They prioritise wider business success above their personal interests.

This may seem obvious, but in our experience it is far from common practice. We have witnessed many meetings where leaders, particularly at the top of organisations, struggle to suspend their own interests. More often, we notice leaders being inflexible, defending the interests of their own function, country, region or business unit.

A clear sense of purpose helps develop a sense of duty. The 'connectedness' to something greater than oneself fuels motivation. Connectedness reflects the sense of unity with others and helps develop relationships based on mutual trust, support and understanding. Such connectedness provides a direction for you to exercise your sense of duty.

Leaders of character understand that satisfaction and motivation depend not merely on having goals, but on having the right goals. They need to see that their work has meaning and that they are contributing to the growth of the business and its place in society. They feel a strong sense of connection to what their organisation stands for and are prepared to bring discretionary effort to work every day.

A number of the leaders we know who exemplify this behaviour gain valuable perspective on the meaning of their work, perhaps paradoxically, through the work they do outside their organisation. Many serve on community associations, boards of charities, run sports teams, are magistrates or chair of the school governors. This is not for everyone but what it brings is an opportunity to practise leadership in a non-work environment, whilst making a broader contribution to the community. The leader's work is enriched as a result and the business benefits in the long run.

So how can you start to think and act outside of your own self-interest? You can believe, think, say, do and ask yourself.

BELIEVE

This is really powerful: what is your purpose? What do you believe you are on Earth to accomplish? Having a clear and fully formed belief about your purpose is honestly like rocket fuel. It guides how you work, how and what you do, what you don't do and simplifies making decisions about how to contribute to the greater good. Spend time working out your purpose and witness the impacts on your drive and commitment. Incredible!

THINK

A clear sense of duty relies on clarity of purpose. Once you have established the latter, the former is guided within the context of the purpose you are striving to achieve. You can check your thinking and decision making against this touchstone. Any judgement calls, whilst still possible to get wrong, are at least based on a sense of what is right for you, what you deem to be right for others and for your wider organisation.

SAY

Once you have crafted your purpose, it is important to hear how it sounds. Get feedback from friends on whether the way you have constructed your purpose resonates as a fair reflection of how they see you. Does it fit? Continue to shape it.

Practise saying it when you are asked about it. Also, you can try volunteering more at work. Is there a project no one else wants but you recognise as important? Speak up and volunteer to lead it.

DO

Here are three ways to bring a sense of purpose to your leadership role.

1. The next time you have a decision to make, consider the broader impact and implications of the options you have available:

   - What is the challenge or issue?
   - What choices do you have?
   - What are the potential consequences, the pluses and the minuses of each of these choices?
   - Given your sense of purpose, which of these choices appears most attractive to you?

Look beyond your own needs and take time to consider the wider impact of your leadership. Consider drawing others into the decision-making process. Counter-intuitively, the clearer your purpose, the quicker decisions get made. So, bringing others into the process won't slow it down and a better decision should result.

2. Widen your influence and your service. Seek out opportunities to volunteer your services in the community. Become a mentor to someone at work who typically might not get such an opportunity. Done well, everyone wins in a mentoring relationship.

3. Check out your leadership style. Commit to leading for the good of others who have granted you, formally and informally, the title of leader. Regularly check in with your team members to see how you are doing and what you could be doing even better.

ASK YOURSELF

1. What is my purpose? To help with the process, consider:
   - What do you like most about work?
   - What does it mean to you?
   - Why is it important?
   - When are you most fulfilled at work?
   - What has been the most enjoyable moment in your work? Why?
   - When are you at your best? What is going on for you?
   - What do you never want to give up?
   - What are you in this role to do? Why is this important to you?

2. As a business leader how can I further help my team, peers, boss and customers?

3. What are my values? How do these relate to my purpose? In what new ways could both be better served?

4. What are my goals for the coming year? How do they connect to those of the business?

5. What it would be like to be a model corporate citizen in my organisation? How can I hold myself to that account?

HELPING OTHERS

5. I focus on helping others to make their very best contribution at work. Or put another way: it's not about you.

Leaders of character know that it is care for the work and the people in the business that makes the difference between success and failure. People want to follow a leader who cares about all the people involved in the effort, not just the targets that need to be met. Real leadership strength is measured by what leaders enable their followers to achieve. Selfless leaders get their egos out of the way in order to focus on the mission and, most importantly, those who deliver it.

Writing in *Sacred Hoops* (find a copy and read it cover to cover), Phil Jackson, former basketball coach to the Chicago Bulls and LA Lakers, winner of 11 NBA titles, talks about his personal crusade against selfishness – where players were more concerned with personal performance and brand enhancement, rather than the team's success.

In the early weeks at Chicago, Jackson was credited with getting the best out of the world's greatest player (in our opinion), Michael Jordan. Following yet another lost match, albeit one where Jordan had been top scorer and star performer, Jackson told Jordan: 'The sign of a great player is not how much he scores, but how much he lifts his teammates' performance.' The rest, as they say, is history.

Sport is littered with examples of people sacrificing themselves to the team ethic. The goal of every All Black rugby player is to contribute to the team's legacy by doing his part to keep the team progressing every single day. No one is too big or too famous to do the little things required each and every day to get better.

Whether in sport or business it would appear that Robert Greenleaf's views on servant leadership going back to the 1970s still ring true:

The best test, and difficult to administer, is: do those served grow as persons? Do they, while being served, become healthier, wiser, freer, more autonomous, more likely themselves to become servants?

Easy to say, more difficult to do.

So how can you become more selfless in pursuit of a common cause? You can believe, think, say, do and ask yourself.

BELIEVE

The real challenge with selflessness is that we have an in-built survival mechanism to put ourselves first. Whilst that makes sense, it doesn't play out very well in organisational life. Believing that practising selflessness is worth doing is the place to start. Believing that it is possible to put others first, without losing a sense of yourself and your own dreams, is a paradox that is well worth being able to balance.

THINK

If selflessness is not natural, then you need to think more consciously about what you do and how you do it. You need to:

- think before you act
- think before you speak
- think after you've acted and spoken.

All this thinking will bring a level of awareness that will help you to check in with what you are doing and ensure it is aligned to a more selfless way of being.

By the way, when you first start practising this, it's exhausting but it is well worth the effort.

SAY

As you bring greater awareness to how you are being, you will notice changes to your patterns of speech. There will be more 'you' and 'we' in your conversations and fewer (although not totally absent) 'I' and 'me'. Start with others. Ask questions of others and explore what they are doing, how they are feeling and find out how you might help.

DO

Here are seven simple ways you can start to lay the foundations of selfless leadership right now:

1. Stop telling and start asking. Show genuine interest and concern for others through asking great questions.
2. Help 'sweep the sheds'. Take your turn to do the dirty work on behalf of the team from time to time.
3. Let others take on the leadership of certain projects. By reversing roles, leaders not only facilitate employees' development, but they model the act of taking a different perspective, something that is so critical to working effectively in diverse teams.
4. Make small personal sacrifices occasionally, such as missing a family event or going into the office rather than working from home, to support someone else's project.
5. Aim to leave people feeling better and stronger as result of time spent with you by asking how they're doing and showing real interest.
6. Make time to coach others in your team.
7. Listen. Listen until it hurts. Play back what you heard.

ASK YOURSELF

1. What would it take for me to be more oriented towards others?

2. How will I ensure that I am truly listening when others speak?

3. How can I ensure I balance my own presence, whilst ensuring others get the limelight?

4. Who can I role-model that seems to do this really well?

5. Where can I start to 'go the extra mile' for others that I have neglected to do so up to this point?

CHAPTER 4
DISCOVERY

INSIGHTS

AN INTRODUCTION TO DISCOVERY

Excellent leaders are constantly challenging themselves to think of new ways to do things and are never content with doing something the conventional way if a better way is possible. They are curious about everything and enjoy exploration and discovery. They thrive on thinking things through in detail and do not jump to conclusions. They seek solid evidence to aide decision making but are able to change their mind in the light of new information. They enjoy learning new things and have a way of looking at the world that makes sense to others. People frequently turn to them for advice.

A BETTER WAY

6. I am not content with doing something the conventional way if a better way is possible. Or put another way: avoid uttering 'We have always done it this way.'

Constantly search for new and better ways to do things – to the point where you become an irritant to some. Yes, people around you would prefer you to stay on the safe ground and repeat last year's approach to budgeting or organising a conference, but leaders of real character lie awake at night thinking that there must be a better way.

By all means review what happened last time around. What worked last time and how can you build on this? What could be done better and how? And recognise that last time around is relevant only to inform learning.

Leaders are pioneers: they are willing to step out into the unknown. They remain open to receiving ideas from anyone and anywhere. They spot good ideas and are willing to challenge the system to get new products, processes, services and systems adopted. They think about 'what if' and 'what's next'. They don't get trapped into a set way of thinking. They remain in constant search of discovery in order to seek new and better opportunities.

This type of creative leader is an early supporter of innovation, knowing full well that innovation and challenge involve experimentation, risk and, even, failure. Experiments don't always work out as planned. People often make mistakes when they try something new. Instead of trying to apportion blame for mistakes, they learn from them and encourage others to do the same. They understand that the key that unlocks the door to opportunity is learning, especially in the face of obstacles.

Exceptional leaders challenge everything – especially conventional thought, best practices and existing practices which drive businesses into a way of thinking that is no longer relevant. Anything in business can be improved and everything can be reimagined.

So how can you develop the mindset for continuous improvement? You can believe, think, say, do and ask yourself.

BELIEVE

Do not fall into the trap of believing, as the old saying goes, 'If it ain't broke, don't fix it.' Failing to continually challenge how things are done will mean that, at best, you will stagnate and, at worst, you will become unable to compete.

Do fix your mindset on these two central beliefs:

- Growth comes through innovation.
- Failure is not something to avoid but embrace.

THINK

If you set your mind to accommodate these beliefs, new thought patterns will emerge. You can encourage such thoughts by reflecting on the following questions whenever you consider a decision:

- Are we playing too safe here?
- Have we mitigated risk sufficiently?
- Have we explored with team members their view of the culture around innovation and especially around failure?
- Am I encouraging my team to come to me with (creative) solutions rather than problems?

Remember, too, to explore constantly how you and your team can refine ways of working to improve efficiency, speed and quality.

SAY

Adapting how you speak will encourage constant improvement. Using verbs (the doing words) adds energy and action-orientation to your communication. Check how you write and speak to see if you employ verbs regularly.

Consider how you respond to failures. Ranting and finger-pointing rarely helps. Acknowledging that such eventualities happen, whilst also looking to help people learn, always helps. Asking questions in a tone of genuine curiosity is the best way to encourage reflection, learning and to ensure the same mistakes aren't made twice.

DO

Here are five time-proven steps to create a culture of continuous improvement for you and your team:

1. Set up a time each week to review your performance as a leader of yourself and your team. Friday afternoon works well for this.

2. Select a member of the team to act as 'Quality Assurance' on each project. This person gets to challenge if there are better ways of doing things.

3. Set up a daily 'Pulse' meeting to see how people are performing and get helpful input from the wider team. Allow 15 minutes maximum per meeting.

4. Break up silos and go with a matrix approach where you can. In other words, mix it up. Encourage working with new people and new areas of the business.

5. Get one person per month to act as your team's in-house researcher. Have five relevant themes they research that will help inform new ways of working.

ASK YOURSELF

1. Does the business model afford me a competitive advantage moving forward or would it benefit from a fresh look?

2. How relevant and timely is the management information produced for or by my team?

3. Does our organisational structure support our business goals?

4. Am I creating the right business culture to support the service strategy?

5. To what extent is my approach to talent acquisition and development fit for purpose?

6. Can I simplify systems and processes in order to make them more effective?

CURIOSITY

7. I am curious about everything, always asking questions and keen to discover new information. Or put another way: 'We don't know what we don't know.'

The curious leader has an insatiable interest in new people, new things and new experiences. They have constantly active minds as one fresh insight leads to another, which leads to the desire for yet further discovery. They pursue this interest for personal growth with a view to uncovering fresh insights and new ideas that can take their team and the business forward. Without an eagerness to discover, there can be no innovation, awareness, problem-solving, value creation or agility.

We were all great at discovering as young children when we saw the whole world as an adventure playground. Yet over time many of us lose this natural instinct – as if exploring and asking questions exposes us as 'unknowing' or inferior. Often it requires courage to ask the dumb question that everyone in the room wants to know the answer to. Get out of your own way and find the confidence to go where others are not prepared to go. Role-modelling such a naïve approach, where you park your ego at the door and seek to discover, has very positive effects on others too.

Todd Kashdan, researcher and author of the wonderful book *Curious?*, recommends always listening to really smart people. Even if they are wrong, we can learn something.

Todd suggests that in your network you have, at the very least:

- one person older than you, who is where you want to be in the future
- one peer who possesses strengths and accomplishments that you don't
- one person younger than you, who is further along than you were at that age.

Noveltyseeking, searching for knowledge and an openness to new ideas and experiences characterise the curious mind. Liz Wiseman argues in her book *Multipliers*, that today's most effective leaders amplify the capability and intelligence of their teams by accessing the collective wisdom of the group. She proposes that the principle role of leaders today is no longer knowing and directing, but rather asking and listening.

How can you cultivate curiosity? You can believe, think, say, do and ask yourself.

BELIEVE

It is possible to develop a discovery mindset, but it requires a willingness to disrupt yourself. So, the first principle to establish is a belief that discovering perspectives, information and approaches that are new to you is truly valuable. Couple valuing such newness with a willingness to acknowledge that formerly held beliefs might no longer be helpful is also key to discovery. You're going to need to let go of the old to embrace the new.

THINK

Can you assimilate fresh thinking easily? Developing the ability to appreciate new ways of looking at the world, and dropping perspectives that are outdated or irrelevant, are signs of advanced thinking and a mature leader. Sometimes you will need to be able to hold seemingly opposing thoughts, such as, 'I don't agree with the new company change programme but, now it has been agreed, I will support it publicly.' Effective leaders can balance such paradoxical thinking.

SAY

If you adopt an inquisitive style of speaking using questions, you are much more likely to find yourself exploring situations with your team members and uncovering their motivations and thinking.

Some really useful enquiry statements and questions include:

- Tell me a bit more about ...
- Can you help me understand some more about ...?
- What are the reasons for that?
- Can you describe that to me as if I'm a beginner?
- What does that mean for us?

DO

Here are five ways to develop a love of learning and exploring new approaches that will cultivate a discovery orientation:

1. Select a magazine or blog in an area that you know nothing about and subscribe to it for six months. After six months, swap to a new source in a new area.

2. Sign up to some podcasts in related and indirectly related areas to your work.

3. Write a weekly newsletter or email to your team exploring what you have learned and asking for your team to offer you advice or to build on your learning with additional insights.

4. Use a daily journal to explore your thinking, established patterns and ways of working with a view to critically reviewing where these have come from, if they are still effective and how you might adapt your thinking.

5. Seek out a mentor who has succeeded as a leader and who would be willing to constructively challenge your current ways of leading.

ASK YOURSELF

Here are some 'go-to' questions to ask yourself that will help you stay curious:

1. Why are we doing this in the first place?

2. What is unknown here?

3. How can I apply this knowledge to my work?

4. What assumptions am I/are we making?

5. What established patterns have I fallen into?

6. If I could think about this situation or challenge in a way that my boss, mentor or leadership hero would, what would I be thinking right now?

7. Am I truly open to the new ideas presented here?

OPTIONS AND EVIDENCE

8. I consider the available options and evidence before making decisions. Or put another way: how to make mind-blowing decisions.

We all know leaders whose thinking is constrained by their past experiences and existing belief systems. They open problem-solving or decision making dialogue around an issue and proceed to steer the solutions towards the one they have in mind. In their view, theirs is the only logical and sound conclusion. Top-performing leaders take a different view:

- They believe that a preparedness to suspend their beliefs in order to take the appropriate account of fresh insights and ideas is critical to the success of the enterprise.
- They look at all the evidence before making a decision.
- They are prepared to revise their opinions as fresh evidence comes to light.
- They value their intuition, particularly where there is a sense of urgency, but recognise its limitations.
- They are able to make informed decisions very quickly.

Often, we encounter narrow thinking in new leaders. They frequently show an over-reliance on their own expertise to make judgements and fail to take account of the hard evidence or the opinions of others. Such leaders were previously valued as individual contributors for providing such expert opinions. Faced with a new team, they can fall back on their expertise in order to earn credibility and bolster self-confidence in their new role as leader. Team members simply may stop contributing ideas and views because they fall on 'deaf ears'.

Sometimes, intuition or a gut feel is sensitive to the finer details of decisions and unearths key information that processes miss. As a result, advocates of intuitive decision making suggest that your intuition reveals elements of a situation that your ability to reason cannot. However, as the world becomes increasingly complex, decisions based on experience or hunch alone will be compromised. Many decisions that leaders face at work today have a greater novelty factor, meaning dependency on prior experience limits your ability to find the best way forward without thorough research.

Simple tactical decisions, where the cost of errors may be low, can still be made through gut feel. This can add speed and free up time and resources to focus on more strategic issues. Where the stakes are high, you will benefit from 'taking time to make time' or face the possible consequences. Research tells us that where decisions are made following rigorous procedures, achieving desired outcomes increases.

So, how can you develop your decision making abilities? You can believe, think, say, do and ask yourself.

BELIEVE

Limiting beliefs held by leaders in relation to decision making include:

■ I have all the answers.

■ I should have all the answers.

■ My credibility relies on me knowing everything.

Top leaders have confidence in what they *do know,* coupled with a willingness to accept that they cannot (and should not) know everything. Establishing what decisions need to be made, and what information is needed in order to decide, enables processes to be followed, resulting in considered decisions and managed risk.

THINK

A willingness to explore what you don't know when big decisions have to be made is a great starting point for leaders. Openness to new thinking develops flexibility in your learning as a leader, which is vital in the current environment. Without hampering speed, also seek to tap into the advice and thinking of others too. Ultimately, some decisions will have to be made by you. Take as much time as you can to consider your options from the available data and then decide.

SAY

Again, questions will be your ally in decision making. Asking questions at a deep level helps ensure you are aware of all available information. This means digging beyond the initial responses you receive so you can test the robustness of the data you are being given.

DO

The next time you face a critical leadership decision, try the following seven steps:

1. Identify a wide range of possible courses of action.

2. Fully research each possible approach.

3. Identify the possible positive and negative consequences of each option.

4. Search for any new missing information or expert opinion relative to each of the options.

5. Assimilate new information accurately, even if it does not support your initial preference.

6. Re-examine all possible future positive and negative consequences.

7. Make detailed plans for implementing the preferred approach.

And here are four actions to avoid when faced with a critical leadership decision:

1. Do not give excessive credence to the first option thought of in the interests of speed or looking smart.

2. Do not favour approaches that support the status quo just to avoid further disruption or change.

3. Do not back options that support earlier choices made, even though they have been shown to be flawed, in order to avoid embarrassment.

4. Do not collect evidence that supports only YOUR preferred option above the ideas of others.

ASK YOURSELF

1. How am I influencing the final option?

2. What else can I do to ensure the decision is as robust as possible?

3. How diligently have I ensured this process has been?

4. What would my line manager say if they reviewed our decision making process at this point?

5. What is stopping me deciding?

6. How can we further manage the risks without hampering the time the decision will take to make?

7. When will I know that we have enough data to decide?

Emotions and decision making

Approaching key decisions whilst experiencing high levels of stress and anxiety clouds judgement. Faced with the choice between conflicting courses of action, you may experience feelings of uncertainty, vacillation and hesitation. You may even sense a strong desire to escape from the dilemma by avoiding making the decision or rushing your decision just to make those feelings go away.

On the other hand, if the feelings you are experiencing around a possible choice are those of ambivalence, you may be less than motivated to give the decision adequate thought. Both mental states call for you to be honest with yourself and recognise those unhelpful feelings, back away, gather new information, involve others, re-evaluate the pros and cons, sleep and eat well, then return with fresh eyes.

LEARNING

9. I encourage others to love learning as much as they do. Or put another way: stay relevant by committing to mastery.

When David started working with a former boss, he was surprised by the boss's tendency to share little insights he had found on the web and handing over copies of interesting books that he had recently read. Intrigued by his insatiable appetite for new information and fresh insight, David lapped up every gem and nugget of information.

Initially, he was overwhelmed by his boss's generosity and desire to share. His boss's view, though, was that it gave him pleasure to pass on something that he had found useful to someone whom he sensed might find it useful too. Underneath this transaction existed a love of learning that David's boss wanted to encourage in David and intuitively knew he would value.

In fact, it became a habit that David adopted with people who later looked to him for leadership. No one has ever responded negatively to this approach, whether sharing a book, an article, a ticket to a seminar or an introduction to a new person who may have insight on an issue. The fact is, most people find learning and getting better at what they do motivating.

The feelings associated with increased levels of competence and knowledge fuel growth and confidence in work performance. Similarly, new challenges offer the opportunity to learn and grow, and effective leaders are always on the lookout for opportunities to stretch their people and encourage the pursuit of those small changes that make a difference to their performance. This two-way relationship between challenge and learning is something great leaders understand and it creates opportunities to exploit. It is a classic case of success breeding success.

For us, systems scientist Peter Senge hits the spot with this thought on personal mastery:

> *People with a high level of personal mastery live in a*
> *continual learning mode. They never 'arrive'.*

Sometimes, language such as the term 'personal mastery' creates a misleading sense of ownership. But personal mastery is not something you possess. It is a process, a lifelong discipline.

How can you develop personal mastery? You can believe, think, say, do and ask yourself.

BELIEVE

Whilst many leaders tell us that they have always loved learning, some only catch the bug later in life. We work with many leaders who, following less than stellar times at school, college or university, matured later in life to the positive belief that learning is valuable, fulfilling and is life-affirming. They recognise too that learning is a proven way to ensure they remain relevant to their organisation and can continue to add value. No matter what your experience is of learning, believe that learning is worth it, knowing it is never too late to begin or restart your learning journey.

THINK

Inform your approach to lifelong learning by acknowledging its importance for you and your career. Here are some things to reflect on in relation to your thinking about learning:

- Review what informs your current thinking about learning.
- Consider how you role-model learning to your team and peers.
- Reflect on what mindset changes you could make to be a more fully engaged learner.

SAY

Talking about your own learning experiences – past and present – can help your team and peers be more open about some of their experiences too. Such openness establishes the space and trust needed to discuss how to broaden the learning that happens in your organisation. Ask your team how they learn best and explore ways to enable learning in your organisation, including less formal methods, such as learning on the job or from action-learning groups.

DO

Here are five easy ways to develop a culture of learning and mastery:

1. Develop your skills as a coach: a core leadership skill in helping adults learn. See insight 43 about coaching in Chapter 11 for more details.

2. Encourage members of your team to give each other regular feedback around what they do well, how they can build on this, what they could do better and how.

3. Set up reverse mentoring where someone junior on the team, with relevant and useful insights, mentors a more senior person who is keen to learn – a junior female mentoring a senior male leader, focusing on gender.

4. Seek opportunities for you and your team to take in-house secondments or join project teams. Ensure knowledge gained is shared with the team on return.

5. Set up a learning log – have a WhatsApp or Slack (app) group that captures what you have learned each week. This quickly becomes very motivating and has an intrinsic value.

ASK YOURSELF

1. What learning can I take from this experience?
2. When do I create specific time in my week to learn?
3. Which members of my team would benefit most from this information?
4. Who could be my leadership mentor?
5. On what topics could I effectively mentor members of my team?
6. What topics am I closed to learning about? What are the reasons for being so closed? What am I willing to do about it?

INSIGHT

10. I provide valuable insight on matters and have a way of looking at the world that makes sense to others. Or put another way: it's all a matter of perspective.

Understanding how you see the world is vital to great leadership. In fact, we think that understanding your own perspectives in some fundamental areas is critical to developing yourself as a human being, let alone as a leader.

YOUR WORLD VIEW

How you look at some key areas of life has an impact on your approach to change, other people and your own development. Your perspectives even affect how you view fundamental things such as knowledge, truth and human nature.

Just a few of the areas that affect the shape of your own world view, and that are highly relevant for leaders to consider, are set out in the table below as opposing pairs. It is adapted from work by Freud and Jung on what they termed *Weltanschaaung* (world view).

Free will	vs	Determinism
You are in charge of your own destiny		There is a 'grand plan' that determines your future
Nature	vs	Nurture
Talents are born, not developed		Talents are made, not born
Uniqueness	vs	Universality
All humans are unique		Humans have traits that can be recognised or labelled
Equilibrium	vs	Growth
Humans resist change		Humans embrace change
Optimism	vs	Pessimism
Humans are positive		Humans are negative
Interdependence	vs	Intradependence
Humans rely on others		Humans are self-reliant

If you imagine each term in the table represents the end of a sliding scale, you can begin to get a sense of how you developed your own world view.

If you feel human beings have full control over our futures and the directions we can take, then your world view is informed by a sense of free will. If, on the other hand, you feel that there is some grand plan and you have a pre-determined destiny, then your world view is informed by a sense of determinism.

You can understand why taking different standpoints shapes your thinking about key areas such as planning, goal-setting, long-term thinking and forecasting.

Knowing how you view the world provides some self-awareness and allows you to seek new perspectives. Perhaps, more importantly, it enables you to know the 'perspective' traps you may fall into because you have certain blind-spots. Once you know this, you can seek complementary and opposing perspectives in order to balance your own thinking.

How can you ensure your way of looking at the world is balanced and makes sense to others? You can believe, think, say, do and ask yourself.

BELIEVE

Believe that there is no 'right' or 'wrong' world view. Such a belief is what allows people to be tolerant of others, embrace difference and avoid bigotry. Brilliant leaders can hold their own world view whilst being deeply appreciative of the world view of others. Believing that they can adapt allows leaders to develop an identity that balances integrity with openness to new and sometimes challenging perspectives.

THINK

Your world view has been formed from a range of significant people in your life and the experiences you have had so far. It is also the product of your willingness to reflect and think about why you view the world as you do. Consider who has influenced your world view and whose world views you would like to be influenced by.

SAY

Being willing to genuinely explore different perspectives is a trait of effective leaders. The leaders who make the most impact who we have worked with excel at wanting to understand and encourage others to share and challenge. They use phrases such as:

- That's interesting – what makes you say that?
- Here's my perspective but I would love to hear others.
- How else could we look at this?
- What are we not considering?
- Have we considered all possible angles on this?

DO

Here are eight ways to develop a balanced perspective:

1. Take into account everybody's perspective more regularly when considering decisions or plans. Be sure to ask 'Have we considered alternatives, the views of customers, employees, managers and all other stakeholders?'
2. Review your own world view, with reference to the table above.
3. Analyse which of your views work well for you.

4. Analyse what views might be holding you or others back.

5. Identify what you can do to adapt.

6. Ask a peer for some feedback about where your perspectives are adding value as a leader and where they might be holding you or the wider team back. Plan how to develop.

7. Find someone who holds very different views from your own – you'll know who they are and you probably don't see eye to eye very often. Ask if you can buy them a coffee occasionally. Chat, be open and learn.

8. Immediately start to encourage a wide range of your team and peers to be involved in key decisions and discussions.

ASK YOURSELF

1. What myths from my past am I holding on to that are no longer true to the way I see the world now?

2. Who are my closest friends? What do I notice?

3. If I could change one view I hold about other people, what would that be?

4. What people do I find it more difficult to relate to or build rapport with? What are the reasons for that?

5. To what extent do I think that I am capable of changing some fundamental beliefs I currently hold as true?

CHAPTER 5
PERSPECTIVE

AN INTRODUCTION TO PERSPECTIVE

Strong leaders have an appreciation of the good things that happen and never take them for granted. They always take their time to express their thanks. They are positive about the future and believe that their performance is controllable. They see the light side of challenging situations. They appreciate excellence and skilled performance in all domains of work. They have strong beliefs about the higher purpose and meaning of their work.

GRATITUDE

11. I am a grateful person, who takes the time to express thanks for a job well done. Or put another way: develop an attitude of gratitude.

Since pre-history, people have devoted much time to being grateful for things that have happened in their life. Prayer, philosophy and actions have demonstrated an almost innate awareness people have – religious and secular – for the importance of developing a grateful mindset. More recently, researchers have also been showing an interest in the importance of gratitude. The evidence suggests that being truly thankful as a generalised way of living, as a trait, improves wellness and health. Genuine gratitude provides significant positives.

A key idea here is that your gratitude needs to be *genuine*. If you finish reading this insight and adopt a deeply thankful approach in all areas of your life, but that only lasts for the next 48 hours, we're not convinced it will make that much difference.

Begin to see the positives in events and situations that you may have been taking for granted and adopt that approach over the long term – and who knows what benefits might accrue? Moreover, faking gratitude is very transparent to others, who will see your new-found attitude as a form of manipulation. Done well, recognising others for their work is incredibly motivating.

You know the concept of unconditional love? It's the sort of thing that an effective parent gives to their child. The idea is not to provide love in return for something, such as good school grades, but unconditional love is unshakable, regardless of what a child does. Likewise, being grateful unconditionally is where you will make the most gains both for you and others. Therefore, avoid using gratitude in the following ways:

- Only when someone has delivered for you.
- Only when you want something from someone else.
- Only when you remember to do so.
- For some people in your team and not others.
- As a way to make people feel indebted to you.

How can you develop genuine gratitude? You can believe, think, say, do and ask yourself.

BELIEVE

A couple of core beliefs that will enable you to adopt a broad attitude of gratitude are as follows:

- Giving recognition and expressing gratitude to people is not in limited supply. You can provide as much of them as you want and as others need.
- Being grateful to others does not make you weak. Lots of leaders start by thinking it does. It doesn't. Showing gratitude is not about you. It is about the recipient.

THINK

Notice how you think when you are debating with yourself whether or not to show gratitude to someone. Is there a little voice in your head saying things like:

- I'll say thank you when they deliver work next time.
- They get paid to deliver. I'm not thanking them for doing their job.
- I need to keep them hungry. Thanking them will make them soft.

If these thoughts sound familiar, you'll do well to challenge them at source. Replace them with some thinking that sees gratitude as good for the recipient and for you too.

SAY

The better you know the members of your team, the more able you will be to demonstrate gratitude in a way that works best for them. For example, some people like to be thanked in a bit of a public display, such as a team meeting, whilst others prefer a private word of thanks. A written word of thanks, not an email, for a very special piece of great work can be really powerful.

DO

Here are four ways to cultivate genuine gratitude:

1. Review all the areas of your life for which you could or should be grateful. Start small – even if only you know you are doing it – and find ways to show thanks.

2. Self-evaluate your performance with your team and peers. Perhaps get some feedback from them too. Are there times you could have shown more genuine gratitude for their support? Where you can admit to mistakes, can you make things right the next time?

3. Check yourself: when are you being grateful *conditionally*? At times you will be. We all are. Reflect on why you and with whom you tend to give conditional gratitude and then work out how to replace it unconditionally.

4. Gratitude comes in many forms. Whilst you may be truly grateful for having enjoyed a wonderful life and family, you are unlikely to be found giving daily thanks for it. Perhaps we all should start to do that? Starting a daily or weekly gratitude journal is a really helpful tool – on paper or via an app. Simply keep a note of something you want to express gratitude towards as and when it occurs and then review at the end of each week.

ASK YOURSELF

1. What informs my current view of gratitude? Is it time for an upgrade of thinking?

2. What concerns me about showing gratitude to others?

3. What assumptions am I making about gratitude that may be unhelpful?

4. What do I feel when faced with an opportunity to give thanks to someone?

5. What would people outside of work say about my spirit of gratitude? How does it compare to when I am at work?

HOPEFULNESS

12. I am hopeful and encourage others to see a positive future. Or put another way: forward-looking hopefulness is a leadership imperative.

Leadership researchers Jim Kouzes and Barry Posner tell us that leaders can leave a lasting legacy, only if they can imagine a brighter future, and that the:

capacity to imagine exciting future possibilities is
the defining competence of leaders.

People want to follow leaders who are positive about the future – leaders who can clear the 'fog' and are not weighed down by the past.

If a leader displays genuine confidence during times of change, it helps generate positive moods and hope in others. Through taking a positive approach, we make a choice to shift our attention away from the causes of problems and direct it towards a clear-eyed concentration on strength, vision, solutions and possibility.

When we are hopeful, we are able to think clearly about possible routes forward to a successful outcome and sustain the energy and drive required to deliver on those outcomes. It is this clarity of 'positive forward looking' that distinguishes leaders of character from others at times of change.

Optimism and hope are similar but different. Whilst optimism correlates strongly with measures of hope, one does not necessarily lead to the other. Whilst optimists may have high will power to change, they may lack the ability to think clearly and analytically enough to be able to determine the best path forward. Leaders, who score high on hope scales, develop clear goals and are continuously thinking about possible ways to attain them. They demonstrate the ability to think critically about ways to achieve their goals, rather than relying on an optimistic belief that things simply will work out.

In tough times, it is essential for a leader to retain faith that they will succeed in the end, *and* they must be prepared to confront the harshest facts of their current reality.

So how can you stay hopeful no matter what? You can believe, think, say, do and ask yourself.

BELIEVE

Whilst optimism is good, adopting a belief based on hope underpins more of an action-oriented approach. Remaining grounded in reality is an accompanying belief that is useful: being hopeful and having a positive outlook is not the same thing as taking a naive Pollyanna view that everything is great. Leaders who are hopeful are realists, so keep a check on beliefs that you are holding to ensure they are reflecting the facts of a situation rather than how you wish it to be.

THINK

Base your thinking in as objective a view of a situation as you can. Hope is not blind to the reality of circumstances. Thus, ensure you challenge yourself to get a full picture of the current reality and then remain positive about your chances of finding ways to uncover solutions. Tap into your own creativity of thinking as well as the thinking of members of your team.

SAY

Introduce the phrase 'I'm hopeful that ...' as this is a powerful way of remaining realistically positive about outcomes. Self-check words and phrases you use that are either negative or overly positive and unrealistic.

Whilst avoiding becoming the 'thought-police' for your team, you can gently challenge language that others use too. Here are some words/ phrases that should set alarm bells ringing:

hopeless, pointless, insurmountable, disheartened, waste of time, impossible, intransigent, can't get them to change and this can't be done.

DO

Here are three ways to remain hopeful, no matter what:

1. Examine your current top three priorities. Identify what attitude you are bringing to these. Adapt your approach where required to reinforce hopefulness.

2. Before your next team meeting, consider how you want to communicate in order to reflect a greater sense of hope: select two or three key messages you want to communicate. Then spend 10 to 15 minutes on each message and consider how to add greater hopefulness. Ensure that you have time for working on solutions within the meeting.

3. Change how you publish meeting agendas:

- Publish your next agenda at least a week ahead of time.
- Frame the agenda as a set of questions rather than items.
- Include desired outcomes from each question.
- Inform the team they will be expected to contribute to finding solutions to the questions in the meeting.
- During the meeting get each person to share some ideas early, so that everyone's voice is in the room. No one gets to hide and no one gets to dominate the airtime.

ASK YOURSELF

1. What do I notice about the times when I display more hope than when I display less? How do I feel? How do others react? What outcomes evolve from each approach?
2. When am I at my most positive?
3. How can I encourage others to be more hopeful?
4. How can I more fully tap into the thinking, insights and motivations of the wider team to drive a solution focus?
5. Who in my team is in most need of some positive challenge around the negative attitude or mindset that they display? How will I positively challenge such behaviour?

THE LIGHTER SIDE

13. I like to laugh and encourage others to see the light side where appropriate. Or put another way: lighten up a bit!

Lighten up. Seriously. We mean it …

We all know you are incredibly busy and that you are doing great and vital work. But, creating a monastery-like team environment, where there is an absence of fun, only works well for monks. Mind you, lots of monks seem to like a laugh too.

Allowing yourself some space for levity with your team at work has the proven potential (Hughes and Avey, 2009) to bring about transformational changes in those you lead, including:

- positive emotions of both you as the leader and those you lead
- improved trust

- greater identification with the direction of the team
- increased affective (psychological) organisational commitment
- improved job satisfaction

Your appropriate use of humour also has a positive impact on creativity and innovation across your team. This may not surprise you. If the boss plays the fool at times, what is often referred to as the 'free child' state, then people tend to relax a little and that is the very best state to tap into creativity and innovation.

Humour, like beauty, is in the eye of the beholder. It is highly subjective. It is this subjective nature that makes leaders nervous about humour. Indeed, getting it wrong and using aggressive humour or thinly veiled bullying via humour can produce all sorts of negative impacts (Pundt and Hermann, 2015). With these cautionary notes ringing in their ears, leaders quite rightly don't want to offend others, so, rather than risk doing that, they create a sterile, monotonous environment at work. And that's a shame and it seems unnecessarily safe.

Whilst we're definitely not suggesting you need to take on the role of team clown or start each day with a little bit of stand-up, it is worth noting that transformational leaders embrace, indeed they seek out chances to see the funny or lighter side of life. They don't contrive it. They don't cross the line and end up being offensive. They just have a light, humour-related energy that is able to see the funny side of things, including themselves.

How can you inject the right balance of levity into your leadership style? You can believe, think, say, do and ask.

BELIEVE

A helpful set of beliefs in relation to humour centre on your views of work and your role as the leader. Here are three beliefs to adopt:

- Being a leader isn't about controlling others.
- Work is where many people spend most of their working hours each week and therefore it is a central part of their (and your) experience of what life is all about. You can shape that experience.
- Levity is an enabler of outstanding performance, not an inhibitor.

THINK

Understanding your mindset around fun, laughter and joy is a helpful start. Exploring how you view these things in the workplace helps you understand why you view things as you do. We have found that leaders who can balance taking their work incredibly seriously with a lightness of touch succeed. Achieving such a blend starts with understanding this balance and holding it as a conscious thought about how you will lead yourself and others.

SAY

Situations where you can demonstrate levity are so specific that it is hard to suggest words and phrases you can employ. However, what you can do is smile and laugh more. When a situation is genuinely funny or ridiculous and it moves you to laughter, lighten up and let others see your enjoyment of the moment. The energy both in the moment and beyond increases significantly with shared times such as these.

DO

There is a case for suggesting that the world is so serious that we seem to have lost the ability to laugh. Here are three ways you can tap back into that life-affirming activity:

1. Find some time at home next weekend to watch your favourite comedy film. Indulge in it and relax. Allow yourself just to enjoy it and, if you feel moved to laugh, go for it. Repeat at least once a month.

2. Look for times at work when a situation provides an opportunity to see the lighter side. Appropriately, of course.

3. Occasionally (not every time), when you make a mistake at work, rather than try to cover it up or brush it off, revel in it. Poke fun at yourself. Yes, it takes some courage to do that but it also shows a confidence that allows others to share their 'glorious failures'.

ASK YOURSELF

1. What appeals to my sense of humour?

2. What are safe areas to exploit when the time is right, with some humour at work?

3. What areas should I steer clear of exploiting, such as personal characteristics, personal situations, religion and tragedy?

4. How would I describe my view of engaging in the lighter side of work?

5. What is my team's culture in terms of setting a positively light atmosphere?

AESTHETICS

14. I appreciate the aesthetics of skilled performance in all domains of work. Or put another way: excellence is captivating.

Leaders who develop great performance in their team revel in the achievements, skills and talents of others and go out of their way to show admiration and appreciation. Often, where performance is exceptional, a leader who is strong in this area may be left open-mouthed or speechless, such is the emotional impact that excellence can have on them.

This is a long way from taking the view that it was their job anyway, or that's what people are paid for. Actually, leaders are more likely to be motivated by the achievements and talents of others, rather than seeing them simply as part of the work contract. They show a genuine interest in the outcomes of people's work and the processes that support it.

Leaders actively seek out examples of excellence
in their people and their work.

Great leaders may see beauty in a traditional sense, in design, a piece of writing or marketing, but are often also in awe of ground-breaking systems and processes, creative solutions to problems, a new accounting procedure or new report format. We even know leaders who get genuinely excited about the creation of a new spreadsheet. And no, we are not using humour here.

Equally, leaders may show an appreciation for people who work in accordance with a shared set of values or principles. They recognise and place a high value of virtuous acts and 'goodness' in others. They show admiration and gratitude for those who actually live shared values, over those who only laminate them and place the poster on their office wall.

What is at the root of such an admiration for outstanding contribution or performance? For us it is not about the need to show appreciation for it. Great leaders are simply deeply moved by the exceptional because they recognise the incredible efforts that go into attaining and sustaining such standards. Awesome presentation? Fabulous project management? Incredible product development? It matters not. Leaders simply love exceptional performance, regardless of context.

So how can you experience and show more admiration of excellence in a leadership role? You can believe, think, say, do and ask yourself.

BELIEVE

Do you believe that developing the maximum potential in everyone is a central part of a leader's role? Yes, then make it so. Do you believe that when the strengths, values and motivations of all the people in your team are aligned they can all achieve outstanding work? Yes, then do what it takes to lead your people to achieve the exceptional.

THINK

Avoid the trap of deficit thinking (focusing on what is not right, or not good enough). Instead, focus on what's good, on strengths and what you want to see more of. Deficit-based thinking is draining for everyone and fails to bolster confidence or drive higher performance.

Strengths-based thinking energises people and bolsters confidence and performance. We don't mean that you need to ignore under-performance or congratulate the ordinary. We do mean that you address such situations by focusing on what you want to see more of – rather than what you want to see less of – and on ensuring the momentum that comes with positive reinforcement.

So, whenever someone completes a truly exceptional piece of work, and you will know because you'll be moved by it, be sure to commend them and make clear what it is about that piece of work that makes it exceptional and what it is that others can learn from it. Think too about the best way to show your appreciation. Whilst many people like to be complemented in public, others don't.

SAY

Some of the best leadership conversations, as reported by 'followers', are when a leader shows unadulterated interest in the work someone has just completed. So, the next time you have the opportunity, take the time to have a conversation with an outstanding performer. Flex your curiosity to understand what drives them to out-perform, as doing so can be illuminating for you, uplifting for them and informative for colleagues.

DO

Here are five steps to appreciating the aesthetics of skilled performance:

1. Suspend your ego and accept that others are capable of great work.
2. Accept that even in tough times, when many things can be ineffective or go wrong, there will be pockets of excellence. Go and hunt them out.

3. Listen out for excellence as well as looking out for it. This will require getting out of your office or workspace and getting closer to your team.

4. Notice whenever you have an emotional response to an exceptional performance – in sport, an orchestral piece, a work of art or anything else. Noticing such emotional responses is a good sign.

5. Consider your own performance when you produce great work, as you must regularly as the leader. How do you respond to that?

ASK YOURSELF

1. What do I notice when I witness exceptional performance?

2. In what contexts am I most or least likely to notice excellence? Why is this? What are the impacts for myself and others?

3. What would my team say about my ability to admire excellence?

4. Where do I excel at work?

5. Who can I show some appreciation to today for a truly great piece of work? Team member? Peer? Boss?

HIGHER PURPOSE

15. I express strong and coherent beliefs about the higher purpose and meaning of work. Or put another way: they lead on purpose.

A clear sense of purpose reveals what you were born to do. Once you are aware of your higher purpose, you are able to let go of the need to get too close to details. This leads to faster decision making.

There is nothing new about this insight, in spite of recent musings on the subject, such as Simon Sinek's 2009 TED Talk. Indeed, the central nature of purpose has been expressed since at least the days of the Greek philosophers, through to more contemporary psychologists such as Viktor Frankl and Patrick Hill.

The idea that having a clear purpose is so important has long been recognised, whether it be global in nature, such as a purpose for your whole life, or contextual, such as your defined purpose as a leader at work. Indeed, recently, Patrick Hill has found that spending some time designing a clear global purpose can even increase your lifespan, regardless of your current age. Now, you can't get more important than that, can you?

When we set up a business together, the very first thing we did, along with our fellow directors, was spend time away from the office defining our core purpose. We worked through several iterations and it continued to be refined, but even from those early days, we agreed that we wanted to 'shape the future of leadership coaching'.

Being clear about our sense of purpose acted as a guide for everything we did. It enabled quicker decision making: 'Is what we are about to do shaping the future of leadership coaching?' It also ensured that we engaged with people who can help us achieve our purpose and helped us be more efficient. And it gave each of us a sense of pride in the difference we can make.

So why is defining your purpose so important?

Because it allows you to tweak the rudder of your life – personal and professional – within a known boundary. Depending on the scale of your purpose, it can also provide you with a connection to something bigger than yourself. It provides a reason for being, living, working and striving.

So how can you lead purposefully? You can believe, think, say, do and ask yourself.

BELIEVE

If you believe in a grand plan – that your life is all laid out for you and that you have absolutely no control over your destiny – creating a purpose will hold very little meaning for you.

If, however, you feel that you have some free will and can shape your future, believing in the power of purpose makes sense. So, commit to developing your own purpose. It will serve you and those you lead.

THINK

Consider:

- What really excites and is important to you?
- What are your views of leadership and of employees?
- What are your values?

What do your answers to the questions above tell you about your potential purpose?

Once you have identified your purpose, find a way to hold on to it consciously and stay connected to it. You could embed it into your screensaver or write it down and carry it around in your wallet.

Keeping it in your field of awareness in this way helps guide your thinking and provides a mantra against which to check your decision making too.

SAY

'Is this in line with my/our purpose?' is a question you can regularly ask, in order to align your decisions and retain coherence in your work. Where decisions do not align, don't dismiss things completely, but consider asking: 'How would this need to be in order to align with my/our purpose?' Sometimes things just don't look or feel right until you look at them from different perspectives. Draw in members of your team too and ask them to consider decisions in light of your purpose.

DO

Here are three ways to access your life's purpose.

1. Write down what you see as your current purpose in life. Hint: it probably involves helping people in one form or another and it probably hasn't got anything to do with the amount of money you are going to make.

2. Work on your purpose over two weeks. Go back to it frequently. Try different words or phrases until you get your 'Aha' moment and realise you have found what you are on earth to do.

3. Decide how you are going to fulfil your purpose. What is the vehicle you are going to use to enable you to be living 'on purpose'? It might be your business, your family or something that is currently a hobby.

ASK YOURSELF

1. What is the purpose of leadership? What does this mean for how I will lead?

2. What is my purpose in life?

3. What is the purpose of our team?

4. What steps will help me ensure that I remain aligned to my purpose?

5. What processes can we include as a team to help us work in a coherent way with our purpose?

CHAPTER 6
DETERMINATION

AN INTRODUCTION TO DETERMINATION

Leaders do not shrink from challenge or difficulty. They have a clear sense of what is right and wrong. They work hard to finish what they start and are not easily distracted. Regardless of what they do, they approach it with excitement and energy. They know their strengths intimately and they come to the fore when the going gets tough.

CHALLENGE

16. I do not shrink from threat, challenge or difficulty. Or put another way: stand up and be counted.

Bravery reveals itself in leaders who show a preparedness to act on their convictions – to do what is right and be accepting of the consequences. In this sense, it is not an absence of fear, rather a readiness to act and not be concerned with risks such as losing a job, being criticised, being embarrassed, making enemies or losing status. Leaders face up to the many situations where they are required to act with moral bravery every day.

Be careful not to confuse bravery with foolishness. Brave leaders know they need to guard against recklessness and a predisposition to take risks without having thought through all potential consequences.

Leader bravery has little to do with status, position, title or income. It is deeply personal, regardless of where people sit in the organisational hierarchy. One person's perception of risk may be very different from another's. Bravery is in evidence when a leader, for whom the act feels uncertain (even a little scary at times), performs with conviction. Another leader may not require bravery to take the same action.

STEVE

Steve, the CEO and owner of a small and highly successful tech company, had a little test for himself that he used as an indicator of whether he needed to switch on his 'bravery' button.

When he was about to contribute to a meeting, have a difficult conversation with one of his team or present to the shareholders, he noticed what was happening in his body and made use of the physiological cues. If his palms were a little sweaty and there were butterflies doing acrobatics in his stomach, it was almost guaranteed that he was going to need to step up, be brave and often be direct. Or put another way: he knew he needed to lead.

The best performing leaders see challenges as opportunities to achieve breakthroughs and personal growth. They often do their best work when there's a chance to change the way things are. Maintaining the status quo breeds mediocrity. Leaders seek and accept challenging opportunities to test their abilities. They look for innovative ways to improve the organisation and are willing to experiment and take risks. Since risk-taking involves mistakes and failure, leaders learn to accept the inevitable disappointments. They treat them as learning opportunities.

When followers experience brave leadership, they gain confidence in themselves and their colleagues. They believe they can accomplish something special and often they do. The risks associated with acting may be real or perceived. Leaders assess each situation to determine accurately the nature of risks. How real is this risk? What are the potential consequences of taking this action? And then make a judgement call to act in the interest of their team or the business, even though they may feel anxiety and uncertainty.

How can you lead bravely? You can believe, think, say, do and ask yourself.

BELIEVE

'Is taking this action worth it?' is not the first question great leaders ask when faced with a real challenge. What they tend to ask themselves first is 'Do I need to do something here?' If the answer is yes, they'll assess their options then move right along. Highly capable leaders are led by the deeply held belief that doing the right thing is always the right thing. Failing to act is not part of who they are. It is not in their Leader iD.

THINK

When faced with a challenge do not kick off your thought process by assessing risk. Start by assessing the situation and your ability to meet that challenge. Think through the available solutions. Then, before taking action, assess the risk. This done, act quickly and confidently.

Diagnose	Benchmark	Consider	Plan	Act!
Situation & outcomes	Capability vs requirements	Options	Inc. risk assessment	Confidently & rapidly

SAY

When the time comes to be brave, brilliant leaders rely on stock phrases, including:

- Yes, we can …
- How can we do this?
- What do we need to do first?
- Who can help us?
- I believe …
- That's just not right. What do we do about it?
- How difficult can it be? (Our particular favourite.)

DO

By stepping into the 'arena of anxiety', leaders take the tough route but know that the most likely outcome is change and learning. By doing nothing and choosing 'creative avoidance', you get to live with the status quo at best. Here are five ways to take action that might make your palms sweat a bit but where real change could be achieved if you step up:

1. Pick out the one tough conversation that you have been avoiding. Make it happen.
2. The next time a mistake happens, accept the blame rather than looking to deflect it and commit to making it right.
3. Stop a situation to address disrespectful or rude behaviour.
4. Find a hobby, project or challenge where you are going to have to really push yourself beyond your current perceived limits: join a public speaking group, run a marathon, live abroad and only speak the local language or call someone who you want to mentor you.

5. In the words of Eleanor Roosevelt, former First Lady of the USA: 'You gain strength, courage and confidence by every experience in which you really stop to look fear in the face. You are able to say to yourself, "I have lived through this horror. I can take the next thing that comes along." You must do the thing you think you cannot do.'

ASK YOURSELF

1. What one thing have I been avoiding that would be good to do now?

2. What is really stopping me from doing the above?

3. Excluding feelings of 'busy-ness', how stretched do I really feel on a daily, weekly and monthly basis?

4. What job would I be doing if I could do anything? Hint: you probably can get much closer to this than you currently think.

5. How would I feel if I was more willing to challenge myself, others and situations, rather than just letting things pass?

RIGHT AND WRONG

17. I have a clear sense of what is right and wrong and shape my actions accordingly. Or put another way: there are reasons why great leaders are high on integrity.

Do you ever feel uncomfortable with what you are being asked to do at work? Are you aware sometimes that the way your boss treats people is certainly not the way you would (or will) do it when you are in their seat? Well, that internal alarm system is linked to your sense of integrity. Living with integrity is about how closely you act consistently with your values.

Here are the top 10 reasons why you should lead with integrity:

1. Leaders who are clear about their values, and spend time being specific about which values they hold as priorities, are easier to follow.

2. Knowing your own values as a leader helps build consistent high-performing teams. If you act consistently, people will experience you in a way that is more predictable – that gives others high levels of certainty.

3. Working in an integrated way with your values reduces the energy required to make important decisions.

4. Whilst your decisions and actions will not always be right, decisions guided by your values can be more readily justified – to yourself and others.

5. Leaders know their values are linked to their purpose and vice versa.

6. Knowing when it's time to leave an organisation can come more easily to those with high levels of integrity. Your inner alarm system informs you when your values and those of your employer are too far apart to be reconciled and it is time to look elsewhere.

7. When people know you have a clear set of values they tend to adapt their behaviours accordingly – helping both you and them.

8. Greater clarity of your values helps you appreciate the dynamics between you and others who might hold similar or very different perspectives.

9. High integrity is not inflexible. When information surfaces that indicates a review of values is required, highly sophisticated leaders take time to reconsider how they might adapt.

10. Finding a new job is much more straightforward when you are clear on what drives your integrity. You can find a new organisation to work for simply by getting a feel for their values and the integrity between what they say and what they do.

So, how can you lead with integrity? You can believe, think, say, do and ask yourself.

BELIEVE

Counterintuitively, the ability to hold several perspectives is really important to high integrity – even when those perspectives might appear to conflict. Make sure you can verbalise your values clearly to yourself and couple this with regular reflection on alternative views. This deep reflection helps assert your values and reinforces a life of integrity. It also keeps a weather-check on your perspective and allows for a change in values if feedback suggests a change is important.

THINK

Think regularly about your thoughts and actions. Are they aligned with those values you say are important to you? If they honestly are, then you are living a life high on integrity. However, if like many of us, you own up to areas of your life where your ideal 'self' is not a match for your current 'self', then your life is out of kilter a bit and it will have an impact on important areas such as your self-esteem. Think and plan how to get better alignment.

SAY

Leaders with a clear sense of themselves and their values and who live with high levels of integrity are not afraid to state a position: 'I believe that ...' They won't apologise for holding such a position as they appreciate that we're all entitled to a view. However, they will also often be heard responding to something that does not align with theirs: 'That's interesting. Tell me some more ...' They genuinely want information that helps them understand others.

Practise it – it's liberating, fun and you learn a lot too.

DO

The following exercise comes from a dear friend of ours, recognised psychologist and coach, Professor Tatiana Bachkirova.

1. Divide a sheet of paper into five columns.

2. Now add a title to each column in turn:

   ■ 1: Values
   ■ 2: Ideal
   ■ 3: Current
   ■ 4: Integrity score
   ■ 5: Reflections

3. In the first column, make a list of 10 values that you believe are important to you.

4. In column 2, rank order them 1 to 10 in terms of their importance to you. The most important value on this list gets a score of 1 and the least important gets a 10.

5. In column 3, rank order again with how you live these values daily. The value you live most consistently scores a 1 and the value you live most inconsistently gets a 10.

6. In column 4, calculate the differences in your scores between columns 2 and 3. No need for negative numbers here, just the difference, so if you chose 'Honesty' as a *Value* and gave it a 6 in *Ideal* and a 3 in *Current*, then your *Integrity score* in column 4 would be a 3.

7. Finally, in column 5, write some notes to yourself about why you are living some values in a highly integrated way. They'll have a low score in column 4 – and others less so.

ASK YOURSELF

1. What situations do I find cause me the most disturbance to my values?
2. Where have my values come from?
3. When do I recognise that I most easily appear to act in a way that lacks personal integrity? What are the reasons I tend to do that?
4. What values do I hold that might be inconsistent with who I am now?
5. When do I feel most at ease with myself and at my very best?

SATISFACTION

18. I do not get distracted when at work and take satisfaction in completing tasks. Or put another way: persistence is the key ingredient to your long-term success.

In a brilliant article, with the equally fantastic title 'Mundanity of Excellence', Daniel Chambliss (1989) outlined how swimmers become excellent competitors – how they produce 'consistent superiority of performance'. He suggested excellence in swimming was possible with an approach that focused on doing all the little, normal, inglorious things to an incredibly high standard over the long haul.

Note several important things here:

1. The swimmers didn't just turn up. They applied themselves to the myriad of 'little things' that make up great performance. Focused practice is an important element for excellence. The best swimmers applied themselves in a qualitatively superior way to other swimmers.
2. These swimmers didn't do more lengths than other swimmers. They were not present for longer sessions. They didn't suffer from 'presenteeism'.
3. These swimmers practised excellence over a long timeframe – years.

American swimmer Mary T Meagher won three gold medals at the 2004 Olympics and held the view that:

People don't know how ordinary success is.

Her point that excellence comes from consistent, high-quality actions and thinking aligns with our experience that the highest levels of performance are possible in all fields with such an approach, including leadership.

You may well have heard of the concept that being outstanding in any field can be achieved by applying yourself to deliberate practice for 10,000 hours (Ericsson, 1993). Sadly, such research has often been over-simplified or distilled into bite-sized commentary. That debate aside, it appears to be true that outstanding performers practise deliberately with a focus on high quality over the long haul.

Persistence – the ability to apply yourself over longer periods of time when faced with inevitable challenges – is a quality that we deeply admire in top leaders.

To become an awesome leader of others requires consistent persistence. Being determined to carry out the often mundane to a high quality over the long term, and in the face of obstacles, is pretty much the single biggest factor in determining your chances of success.

So how can you become a more persistent leader? You can believe, think, say, do and ask yourself.

BELIEVE

Committing high levels of energy to excellence over a sufficiently long period requires believing in the importance of the outcome. Clarifying the importance of outcomes (or the benefits) enables you to find the deep wells of drive required to commit to the process. Also, appreciating at the outset that the path ahead will include setbacks, whilst believing that overcoming them will be worth it, provides the spur to long-term, high-quality action.

THINK

Positive thinking here needs to be grounded in your belief that the singular pursuit of excellence in your chosen field – leadership – is a noble and worthy end in itself. If you think developing into a great leader is an expectation of others, or something you need to do to get short-term reward, this project is doomed to failure. You'll no doubt do great for a few weeks, then stop. Persistence requires mental strength, based on internal drivers.

SAY

Individual persistence is accompanied more by internal conversations than by what you externalise. Regularly practising some of the following internal statements helps.

Avoid	Replace with
What will others think?	It doesn't matter what others think, I will achieve this.
This is really important to me.	This is really important for me.
This is boring!	I'm pursuing the mundanity of excellence!
I have to do this.	I get to do this.
That'll be good enough.	How can I do this better?

DO

Here are five top tips for building persistence:

1. Be willing to stare hard and objectively at the level of your current performance.

2. Write down the skills, behaviours, thinking and attitudes you can demonstrate to an outstanding level consistently.

3. Write down the skill that you will need to develop to get your performance to the next level.

4. Have a clear sense of purpose as this will keep your motivation fired up sustainably.

5. Commit to developing consistent persistence in your chosen field, in this case leadership, over a long period. Not just six months, or a year, but three, five or even ten years. Persistence has a lovely and helpful relationship with patience.

One further thought about persistence. Grow the capacity to do a lot in a narrow field, rather than a little in lots of fields. Such a focused approach allows you to build expertise that helps you find solutions to challenges more readily when they occur. It also allows you to develop excellence in your chosen area, with the accompanying benefits, such as high levels of self-confidence.

ASK YOURSELF

1. How important is developing X (e.g. leadership) to me?

2. What setbacks can I expect to come along the way?

3. How will I stay on track?

4. Who can I connect with to help me stay focused?

5. What do I find uninteresting even though it is important for me to succeed? What will I do about that?

6. When do I get impatient with progress? How will I make sure I stay the course?

7. When I imagine succeeding it would be like ...

EXCITEMENT

> 19. I approach all work with excitement and energy. Or put another way: vitality is the spice of life.

Vitality is a key attribute to highly effective leadership. Leaders who are truly following their passion and have a clear vision and sense of purpose exude a real energy. We have met many seemingly quiet, even reserved leaders, who come alive as if a switch has been flicked when they are given a platform to engage in a topic that is deeply important to them.

However, there is what can appear at first to be a downside to such vitality. That is that not everybody else is going to be as engaged by your thing as you are. Indeed, your own passion for your thing may come across as vital to some but pushy or overbearing to others.

Let us share an example. Gary Vaynerchuk came to prominence as a very early e-commerce guru in the world of wine. In more recent years, he has set up his own media company and gives keynote speeches all over the world. Here's the thing: Gary's style is so 'in your face' with expletives aplenty that many people can be turned off by him initially. He is strident. He is forceful. But he is also really clear on his message, awesome at what he does and unapologetic about who he is. He appears to have taken his own social filters away and, as a result, has buckets of vitality to spare – including his legendary 18 to 20 hour-long workdays. He inspires so many people through his energy that it is difficult not to get swept up in it, even if you were initially sceptical.

Now, we're not suggesting that you start swearing and ranting at those you lead. Rather, our point is that you get clear on what really drives you. If you can't be vital and alive about an element of your own leadership, there is slim chance you can influence positive engagement with those you lead.

So how can you develop vitality in your leadership? You can believe, think, say, do and ask yourself.

BELIEVE

A deep connection with your purpose and mission will allow you to generate all the vitality you are going to need. Believing that what you are doing is important, both for you and for others (employees, employers, society) will provide bucketloads of drive and energy. A measured belief in your chance of success is also important. Be balanced but don't shy away from your ability to achieve great things – by whatever standard you judge that to be.

THINK

We know many leaders who are constantly asking themselves, 'How would doing this align to my purpose?' If the answer, following some thinking, is that moving ahead is coherent with your purpose, then go right ahead. However, if it isn't aligned, you may be best to take a pass. In addition to checking for such alignment, good leaders also think about 'How can I be my best self in this situation?' They are acutely aware that as a leader they are never not role-modelling to others.

SAY

Say 'no' when you need to.

Experienced leaders say no when asked to do something that is not important to the priorities they are working on. They do not apologise but they do give a short explanation, helpful to others, especially if those others are not used to people saying no. Such an explanation can be as simple as: 'I can't do that at the moment because all my energies are going into …'

DO

Here are five ways to bring more vitality to your role as leader:

1. Check all the work you are currently doing. Find things you can stop doing or pass on to someone else to do. Then dump things or delegate them.

2. Renegotiate some of your work with your line manager so you can focus more clearly on the important work.

3. Start to notice your rhythms. Notice when you do your best work and have the most energy. Focus important work in those times of day or night.

4. Monitor your nutrition. Poor eating habits significantly impact your moods and also the energy levels you have.

5. Break up the day, especially when your work is largely desk-bound. Move around. Not only is that movement a great way to raise your energy level but it allows you to get closer to your team, and that should prove mutually helpful in remaining connected to your purpose and provide plenty of vitality.

ASK YOURSELF

1. How does this work help me achieve my purpose?
2. Can I say no to this request?
3. What can I delegate to others?
4. Is this a helpful food, exercise or habit choice for me, right now?
5. What is the perception of others about how much I demonstrate vitality?
6. How can I demonstrate my passion for this work more obviously but in a way that works for my personality?

VALUING STRENGTHS

20. I value my own strengths and the strengths of others. Or put another way: build on what works best.

Self-awareness is perhaps the single component that every successful leader possesses in abundance. Knowing your own mind, your own strengths and how to access those strengths whenever you need them differentiates the best leaders from the rest.

Being aware of your unique strengths, and having robust confidence in them because previous experiences showed evidence of their existence, enables people to feel self-worth. People who value themselves lead more satisfied lives and contribute more to the world.

You must also spend some of your time focused on what needs improving, of course, so you need to be aware which elements of your performance aren't up to scratch. But giving too much time to your deficits will only lead to you not fulfilling your potential.

Successful leaders recognise the value of increasing their belief that they will be successful at a chosen task in a given situation. They know that playing to their strengths and the strengths of others increases chances of success. They don't take strengths for granted – they look to maximise strengths and find out how far they can take them. They admire and will draw on strengths of others too.

In the spirit of balance, a word of caution feels appropriate here. Bernard Haldane provides us with a necessary reminder that helping people to play to their strengths can be accompanied by danger:

Many individuals would rather not know what is strong about them, the strengths that point to growth and reveal potential [because] a greater degree of responsibility is required to take hold of success rather than to stay in the safe arena of complacency and complaint.

So, how can you take responsibility for success by focusing on your strengths and those of your team members? You can believe, think, say, do and ask yourself.

BELIEVE

There is a fine line here between believing you possess strength in an area and being deluded about your ability. You need high levels of self-awareness to be accurate in your judgement. In many ways, your ongoing development might best be predicated on genuinely believing that building strengths is a never-ending process. Adopting such a core belief is central to continuing the process of growth.

THINK

Thinking about what strengths you possess and the evidence that supports this conclusion is an important first step. 'How can I apply my strengths, or those of others, to succeed here?' is a central question asked almost reflexively by effective leaders to situations they face. They also think about where they have some gaps and if tapping into their strengths can help close those gaps.

SAY

Feedback is vital in developing high levels of self-awareness. Asking others about the strengths you demonstrate effortlessly can provide you with lots of data. Asking people you know if they can share some thoughts with you about the strengths you think you have and the areas you need to develop will give you useful feedback. No need to justify or explain the feedback you get, just thank the person for their time and go and reflect on what you have heard and plan what you are going to do about it.

DO

Here are seven tips for becoming a strengths-focused leader:

1. Seek some feedback on your strengths from others. See above.
2. Ask a range of people to complete the online 360 version of the Leader iD diagnostic, which will generate a huge amount of relevant and specific data about strengths related to your leadership.
3. Identify areas where you are not sufficiently strong. Plan how to develop these.
4. Complete an informal audit of the strengths of people you rely on. Determine times that you might be able to ask for their help to overcome areas where you may be less strong.

5. Find a mentor who has a range of strengths that you do not possess currently and ask if that person will help you develop in specific areas.

6. Take on a challenge that requires you to develop a key area of strength that is a high priority for your current role.

7. Be on watch for strengths that you might over-play. Turning the volume up too high on strengths can turn them into a liability.

ASK YOURSELF

1. Think of one example when you were recently working at your best. Ask yourself what you learnt about your strengths from this experience.

2. When were my energy levels at their highest in the last quarter and why?

3. When is my confidence consistently high and robust? What does this tell me about my strengths?

4. What are the areas of my work performance that I would say are the key strengths I rely upon, and consistently help me achieve?

5. How do I plan to develop my expertise this year?

CHAPTER 7
BALANCE

AN INTRODUCTION TO BALANCE

Excellent leaders often forgive mistakes and always give people a second chance. They are careful people who think things through before acting. They do not seek the spotlight, preferring to let their accomplishments speak for themselves. They consciously regulate what they feel and what they do and are in control of their emotions. Treating all people fairly is one of their guiding principles.

SECOND CHANCES

> 21. I give people a second chance if they have done something wrong. Or put another way: to err is human; to forgive divine.

Have you ever been really disappointed in someone you lead because they screwed up? You put your trust in them and they let you down? You had provided clear guidelines (so you thought) and yet they still managed to miss the deadline or produce something that looked nothing like what you wanted? Annoying, isn't it?

If someone in your team really has performed very badly, there are a couple of ways that you as a leader can react that will be guaranteed to make things much worse.

First, if you fail to be explicit about what was wrong and don't provide the support – either a direction or some coaching – to help the person improve, then you can be fairly certain that similar problems will recur. Don't just cut an under-performer adrift but provide some overt help in order that they improve.

The second unhelpful reaction is never to allow that particular team member to earn back your trust or your respect again. We know that it sounds medieval but we've both worked with a good number of leaders who have told us early in our work together, much less so later, that once someone has let them down, that person is *never* able to earn their way back into the leader's 'good books' to the same degree again. Ever. Woah!

Do you have any idea what the results of such an approach might be?

- People stop taking risks, trying new things and being creative.
- The team stop telling you when they've messed up.
- Members of the team stop respecting you because respect is mutually earned.

Forgiveness isn't a soft and fluffy approach to leadership. Quite the opposite. It is much harder to get over your disappointment (which you are at liberty to communicate, by the way) and still help the individual get better. They will know they messed up, so help them to improve. No one comes into work every day with the express purpose of failing.

How can you integrate forgiveness into your leadership? You can believe, think, say, do and ask yourself.

BELIEVE

Much of the poor leadership response we see in this sort of situation is fuelled by some faulty beliefs:

- Failure is terminal.
- People are letting you down.
- Perfection is attainable.
- High performance can be achieved in a straight line rather than by overcoming lots of bumps in the road.

If you hold any of the above beliefs, you are going to find it hard to forgive, including, by the way, forgiving yourself for failing. Failure happens and it is a great teacher. Start to believe this and practising forgiveness becomes easier.

THINK

Adopt an open, inquisitive mindset. Explore the reasons that a project or a deliverable didn't go to plan. Seek to understand the viewpoint of the person that didn't perform adequately. Think about what you as a leader could have done differently to ensure success. Along with all those involved, think about what learning you can take from the experience to ensure better performance next time.

SAY

The language that accompanies an inquisitive mindset capable of forgiveness is one of questioning. So the next time something goes wrong, ask the person or people concerned:

- What was your understanding of what was required?
- What happened?
- What would you do differently next time?
- What other resources could have made this easier?
- How could I have been more helpful?

Ironically, when you start to ask what *you* could have done differently as the leader, many people realise that the answer is not much and that the accountability sits squarely with them.

DO

Your action in relation to forgiveness is somewhat dictated by opportunities to practise. However, here are some steps you can take to flex your forgiveness muscles:

1. Think about a recent example where you could have shown more tolerance to something that didn't go so well at work or home. Dissect the example and how you responded.

2. Consider how effective your response was in:
   - resolving the crisis in the moment
   - building the performance confidence in the other person for next time
   - taking the learning from the situation.

3. List all the things you will do next time to ensure better immediate and longer-term outcomes.

4. Schedule a team meeting to reset expectations. Be explicit with your team about your approach to people not performing well. Ensure it includes timely, clear and specific feedback, as well as support. Also, agree to create an environment where people feel safe to come and tell you when they have failed to perform appropriately.

ASK YOURSELF

1. How do I view the pursuit of perfection?

2. What is the value of failure?

3. What do I notice happens to me when I perceive someone has let me down?

4. What other ways are there to thinking someone has let *me* down?

5. How open am I to fully trusting someone who has erred?

6. When I failed to deliver in the past, how was that handled by my leader? What impacts did that have on me?

7. What changes will I make in relation to forgiveness?

CHOICES AND CONSEQUENCES

22. I am a careful person who examines all possible choices and consequences before drawing conclusions. Or put another way: take a 360° view, then just decide.

This particular attribute of a leader may, initially, seem at odds with the fast-paced world in which leaders now find themselves. With an ever-increasing rate of change, where the scale of such changes can often be seismic, on first glance prudence seems a little out of a place.

The PR problem prudence has is that it can be used negatively in a way to suggest a leader who is overly cautious or wholly risk-averse. Such definitions represent prudence unfairly. Whilst a leader who is prudent may want a greater depth to the data they have before making a decision, being prudent should not be taken to mean someone who will neither take a risk nor make a decision.

There is a quality to prudence.

It helps balance decision making (and decision makers) that rely perhaps too heavily on gut feelings or who don't, can't or won't get involved in deep levels of exploration and due diligence before making a decision. There is an important difference between being risk-aware and being risk-averse. The latter stifles growth and plays counter to much of the opportunist tendency of leaders. The former is wise and enables risk of any magnitude to be taken, safe in the knowledge that all the available relevant information that could have been considered has been.

An important distinction to make is that someone who is prudent can be so when the situation requires it. They can be said to demonstrate the highly desirable skill of 'contextual prudence'. This is quite the opposite to a leader who is more generally too timid to make a decision. Whilst such timidity may be wholly understandable with some leaders, if they are new or relatively inexperienced, more generally, it is an unhelpful trait. Thankfully, it is something leaders can address with the help of an excellent mentor or experienced leadership coach.

So how can you become more prudent? You can believe, think, say, do and ask yourself.

BELIEVE

Depending on your self-awareness around being prudent, you might need a check to your ego or a boost to your confidence. If you believe your experience and knowledge allow you to make fast and accurate decisions, you may need to accept you don't know it all and more analysis might be prudent. If you know you can delay decision making in order to find that final piece of information, greater self-belief in your ability to decide could prove useful to you and those you lead.

THINK

The mindset required to handle prudence effectively really is one of balance. It is a view that accepts you will never find all the information available whilst also not being overly reliant on gut feel and intuition. Checking yourself, and the mental patterns you might adopt without sufficient awareness, will help enormously to strike a better balance between conviction and diligence when it comes to key decisions. No one likes being led by a complete maverick or a total worry-wart.

SAY

The language around prudence is one that seeks to check the balance of where a situation is at any point in time. One particular CEO we worked with in the utilities industry regularly asked his leadership team an interesting question, 'What don't we know?' It is a good way to help you and others consider some of the areas that haven't yet been explored or have not been sufficiently researched.

DO

Here is a tip that will help you decide in a timely and prudent way.

The major challenge for any leader is knowing when enough information is truly enough, when the depth of detail considered is sufficient. From our days of academic research, we were both advised that exploring the data usually can conclude when the same messages, themes or insights are surfacing. Therefore, once the data is 'saturated', and there is seemingly nothing new to find, then there is probably nothing new to find ... at that moment in time.

And 'at that moment in time' is an important caveat. Many situations are fluid and changing frequently. Therefore testing may need to continue until an agreed point in time, otherwise a leader's research could potentially go on *ad infinitum* and this could lead to a perception from others of being indecisive.

You know when enough is enough, when you are finding nothing new to add.

ASK YOURSELF

1. How comfortable do I feel with this level of information?
2. What more do I need to be satisfied that we have done a sufficient amount of research?
3. When will I know that I have sufficient data?
4. What consequences to this decision have I/we not thought through yet?
5. What is stopping me making a decision?
6. Have I mitigated as many risks as possible?
7. What have I learned that will help me make future such decisions more quickly?

ACCOMPLISHMENTS

23. I prefer to let my personal accomplishments speak for themselves. Or put another way: from humble beginnings ...

Displaying humility without appearing to lack self-confidence is a difficult balance. Showing confidence without coming across as arrogant is equally challenging.

We are both sports fans and particularly love watching athletes and players being interviewed on TV immediately after they have been successful. It gives a valuable insight into their inner workings. In those moments of victory, when emotions run high and guards are down, athletes typically give this range of responses about their success:

- It's all about me.
- It's all about my team and supporters and I don't know how I've managed to win.
- I was really pleased with my 'execution' – the 'in' word of Team GB at the Rio Olympics – and I acknowledge the hard work of all my supporters.

What might leaders learn from such unfettered responses?

The first type of response echoes one we see leaders model often. Teams are just seen as a means to an end, often to their detriment. The individuals who made a success possible are not recognised.

The second type of response is more nuanced. Here, all the glory is given to everyone else other than the leader, whose efforts in organising, motivating and driving the team are left completely unmentioned. In our experience, this can happen for several reasons, including:

- The leader is genuinely aware of how much everyone else has contributed and wants to recognise that.
- The leader lacks some confidence, doesn't like the limelight or doesn't want to raise expectations about how much they can be relied on to produce such great performances again.

The third response is more balanced. Taking such an approach neither overstates nor underplays the role of the leader. The leader is sufficiently confident of the role they played and equally has a clear and overt appreciation of the efforts of the support team. Such an approach works well for leaders because it's just the right thing to do.

So how can you get the balance right between humility and arrogance? You can believe, think, say, do and ask yourself.

BELIEVE

A central idea to having clarity in relation to your levels of humility is what you believe leadership to be about. What is the role of a leader? What is the role of followers? What is the purpose of your team?

These are challenging questions that you will do well to explore. Believing in a two-way relationship with your team is a great place to start. Failing to do so means your resulting attitudes and actions will be out of balance.

THINK

Check your thinking and actions. It is easy to slip too far towards either self-orientation or being overly focused on everyone else:

- Reflect regularly on whether you are recognising the achievements of individuals in your team.
- Think about the current projects and consider who deserves to be recognised for their contribution.
- Next time you get some praise from your boss, once you have thanked them for their recognition, think about who else played a key role and mention them too.

SAY

Say two things.

First, at team meetings – if you mean it genuinely – identify people who have contributed significantly to key successes. Get used to sharing the limelight, even when you know you may have done much of the work too.

Second, when you get praise, don't brush it off but acknowledge it with thanks. Then drop a name or two of other key contributors in there.

DO

Here are three ways to build a culture of humility in your team:

1. Build a team culture where humility about performance and achievement is coupled with an appropriate level of self-confidence. Start by challenging, in a supportive way, how members of your team respond to recognition. If they either over-focus on themselves or on others, you can hold them to the new standards of your team.

2. Consider moving to reward/recognition at a whole team level. This ensures that everyone appreciates that great things can rarely be achieved alone and it keeps you focused on ensuring everyone contributes and everyone is recognised.

3. Personally, ensure you hold yourself to the highest account in terms of your performance. Then it is a bit easier to acknowledge your hard work when you receive praise. You will no longer need to brush off recognition because you can be satisfied you truly gave your best efforts.

ASK YOURSELF

1. To what extent did I do a really great job on this project?
2. Who was instrumental in our success with this outcome?
3. What can I do to share the limelight with those that really deserve it?
4. What does sharing the recognition with others do for my self-confidence?
5. What does it mean to be a leader of other people?
6. How can I build a high performing team?
7. If I were my boss, who should I know about from this team and why?

CONTROL

24. I am disciplined and in control of my emotions. Or put another way: have a word with yourself!

People look up to and respect leaders who are passionate about what they do and who can resist the temptation to 'throw their toys out of the pram' when the going gets tough or when they don't get their own way.

This 'emotional coherence' is, in essence, the state of maximum efficiency and super-effectiveness, where body and mind are one. In this state, leaders are more focused, flexible, clear, energetic and, most importantly, positive. They are in control of their own responses. Such self-control has a positively contagious effect on others.

Neuroscience tells us that when we are under intense pressure we can temporarily lose the ability to think rationally and indeed even our active IQ faculty is reduced. Hence, why being able to control your physical response to pressure is such a key skill set. This ability for self-control is centred on your capacity to regulate your breathing.

Highly successful leaders know that under stress our breathing patterns become erratic and short. We can find ourselves unable to breathe rhythmically at precisely the time we need to most. At such moments, you need to find a way to first recognise what is happening to you and then to take control so that you can return quickly to the state in which you communicate most naturally.

Renowned psychotherapist and researcher Bessel van der Kok advocates the regular practice of yoga for helping with self-regulation. He tells us that its techniques help us to create a rhythm between tension and relaxation, which we can all learn to recognise in our everyday lives. A number of our regular clients, who have tendencies towards volatility (or even hostility) under pressure, have made significant breakthroughs by adopting yoga practices to help with developing self-control.

By finding this emotional balance and increasing our levels of self-control, we can unlock greater intellectual capacity and energy reserves. Physical and emotional lucidity and consistency gives rise to greater cognitive ability, and makes it less likely that our brains will 'shut down' under pressure and lead us to places we would prefer not to go.

So, how can you find such self-control? You can believe, think, say, do and ask yourself.

BELIEVE

Central to self-control is the belief that you can exercise control over yourself. Holding the belief that 'I am short-tempered' is a very different belief from 'I can behave in a short-tempered way.' The former is a static, global and self-limiting view of you. The second suggests a behaviour that shows itself at specific times. The latter position also hints that you might be able to manage and change the way you behave ... which you can, so choose to believe 'I can sometimes' rather than 'I am'.

THINK

Be honest. Do you really want to change your current lack of self-control? If you think you do, great. If you don't have the will to change, you won't. You need to genuinely think this is important, otherwise it is one of the more challenging sets of behaviours to adapt. So, think about:

- Where is my level of commitment to change?
- What am I willing to do to make the required changes?
- What are the benefits of changing? For me, my team, my family ...

SAY

Sometimes a little bit of mental space is the most important thing to improve self-control. Therefore, some great phrases that will help when you need to regain your equilibrium include:

- Can you just give me a moment ...
- I'll need to think that through and get back to you ...

■ It would be good to understand why you say that/why you did that some more so I can think about how best to respond.

DO

Here are three ways to practise improving your self-control:

1. Next time you are in a combustible situation, ask yourself, 'What am I feeling right now?' Do this regularly and you will recognise patterns of physiological signals, such as your stomach churning, your shoulders rising and your face feeling tense. As you become aware of your feelings, you will soon be able to shift emotions, maybe from 'anxious' to 'curious' or even 'excited'.

2. Experiment with consciously shifting your emotions from anxious to curious in the following conditions and note the impacts on the quality of your thinking:

   ■ Quietly, alone, prior to a routine meeting or conversation.

   ■ Quietly, alone, prior to a difficult conversation or meeting.

   ■ In the middle of a routine conversation with others.

   ■ During a high stakes conversation or when a meeting is reaching a critical moment.

   ■ During a conversation or when you are asked a challenging question.

3. Set time aside daily to practise breathing mindfully – say, five minutes a day. Put your hands on your stomach and focus on breathing from the pit of your stomach. If you are doing it right, you will feel your stomach rising and falling, rather than your chest. Count up to 7 on the inhale and 11 on the exhale. You will quickly become more aware of your emotions.

ASK YOURSELF

1. What sort of leader do I want to become?
2. What impact does my current lack of self-control have?
3. What do I notice triggers me to lose self-control?
4. Who do I know who is a really calm leader that might be willing to help me?
5. How committed to change am I?
6. What time will I get up in the morning to practise mindful breathing?
7. How can my family and loved ones help me?

FAIRNESS

25. I treat people with fairness and dignity. Or put another way: human beings first, means of production second.

Do you get anxious about whether you have treated an individual similarly in one situation to how you responded to similar situations previously? Are you a leader who ensures people in your team know where they stand and feel that you are consistent in the positions you hold? If you can answer 'yes' to these questions, then it is likely that fairness is an important value for you. If not, then read on.

The point here is not to ensure that you get every decision 100% correct, 100% of the time. No one can promise that. But what we want to help you understand is why fairness is so critically important to people and why fairness is not the same as equality.

Let's deal with the latter point quickly.

Fairness and equality are not the same. Everyone receives the same salary in a pure meritocracy, on the basis that each person produces exactly the same work for the same number of hours and generates the same value for the organisation. Yet, you know there are people in your team who perform at a consistently higher level than others. To pay them an equal salary to those who are not performing at an equal level is unfair. It would be a case of equality being (markedly) unfair. We are confident that you recognise and reward the better performers differently from those who are not at that level yet. That's fair. Unequal, but fair. Don't confuse the two.

So, why is fairness so important? We seem to be hard-wired to identify unfairness from a young age, but as we get older most of us learn to accept that life throws up inequality from time to time.

When people judge things to be unfair, their neurological response is to provide fewer resources to an important part of the brain called the prefrontal cortex. This results in our diminished abilities to think consciously and in a more complex way. People tend to 'revert to type' when threatened by unfairness, which is not a great platform for high performance. Finding ways to increase the sense of fairness across your team improves trust in you as a leader and raises engagement with those that follow you.

So, how can you increase a sense of fairness across your team? You can believe, think, say, do and ask yourself.

BELIEVE

Striking a balance between consistency and fairness is difficult. Exceptional leaders believe in following organisational policy consistently, in combination with a pragmatic view of the world. There is a belief that, whilst consistency is vital for avoiding anarchy, each situation should be dealt with on its merits. Leaders appreciate that adult professionals have the ability to discuss, negotiate, even disagree fundamentally, and yet do so in a way that retains effective relationships. Taking time to ensure fairness is important to effective leaders.

THINK

When leaders are faced with difficult situations, especially where staff are concerned, they tend to think about what an 'ideal' solution would be – one that works for everyone, is fair and displays consistency. They empathise and project what any proposed course of action would be like, from the view of those involved. Being just and fair is central to the solutions they seek.

SAY

Leaders of character employ internal dialogue to check how to proceed fairly:

- What did I do last time?
- How would this solution be for X, Y and Z?
- What are the pros and cons for all involved?

Leaders of character also 'sense-check' their internal chatter with others:

- How did you feel about this when we did it last time?
- Last time we did X, I'm proposing we do the same now. Are you happy with that?
- I'm keen to make this work for you and [the other person concerned]. Within the constraints we face, what would you like to see happen?

DO

Here are five things you can do immediately as a leader to avoid a meltdown amongst your team members by ensuring that you are being, and being perceived to be, fair:

1. **Do your due diligence:** ensure you preview decisions and review your actions so that you are being consistent wherever possible.

2. **Communicate:** where you can, explain clearly your decision-making process so recipients understand why you ended up at your conclusions.

3. **Share decision making where possible:** get the team to contribute to decisions where appropriate – it helps engagement and provides insight into the process that was taken.

4. **Be open to the fact that you will get it wrong:** you are a human being. You will get things wrong from time to time.

5. **Provide feedback often:** it is unfair for people that you lead to be unaware they are not performing at the standard that you need them to. If there are technical or behavioural issues, it is fair of you to provide clear, timely, action-oriented feedback for that individual.

ASK YOURSELF

1. Am I trying for equality here when fairness would be a better result?

2. What can I do here to ensure all parties feel fairly treated?

3. What feedback do I need to provide and to whom?

4. How fairly do I treat myself?

5. To what degree is this action consistent with how I formerly acted?

6. What would be the ideal solution for all parties here?

7. What might X be feeling right now?

PART 3

CORE INSIGHTS RELATING TO EXCELLENCE

CHAPTER 8
EMBODIES EXCELLENCE

AN INTRODUCTION TO EMBODYING EXCELLENCE

Outstanding leaders are committed to building a culture of high performance in their teams and constantly strive to get better at what they do. They set a personal example for others of what is expected in the organisation by living and being a champion for the values. They act with integrity and deliver on their promises and commitments. They have clear guiding principles and beliefs about their own leadership and always behave ethically.

SET AN EXAMPLE

26. I set an example by constantly striving to get better and better at what I do. Or put another way: you've got to be able to walk the talk.

We believe that healthy competition is … well … healthy! We also think that there is a place for healthy competition within leadership. Leaders who are highly valued by their organisation appreciate how to use competition productively. They can apply competitiveness in thoughtful ways to maximise its power and manage its more destructive elements. Such leaders are also clear about the area where competitive drive can be directed very powerfully. Namely, towards themselves in the context of their leadership.

UNHEALTHY COMPETITION

Two key areas can be described as the 'dark side' of a competitive nature. First, there is the 'win at all costs' mentality. Second, there is the eternal trap of falling prey to perfectionism.

It is far too simplistic to suggest that the global banking crisis of 2008 was caused by a single factor. What has become clear is that there were failures of leadership. It is also clear that organisational cultures in many banks led to a 'win at all costs' approach, where short cuts were taken, honesty was put on the back burner and people were ignored who should have been listened to. Avoid the allure of short-term gains.

The other trap to be aware of is that of falling prey to competing to be perfect. Nothing is perfect. Lots of things are excellent. So, aim for excellence – it is enabling. Perfectionism is disabling. The former helps you strive towards great performance. The latter eventually leads to giving up, never being satisfied or delivering results too slowly. Compete to be excellent not perfect.

Your number one competition = you!

Whilst you can set up competition with pretty much anything or anyone, there is only one place where you need to focus your competitive nature: yourself. There are many places you can compete with yourself to be better tomorrow than you were today:

- relationships
- results
- effectiveness of your team
- efficiency
- role-modelling being a great leader.

Here is something we have said repeatedly to groups of leaders that produces a previously under-appreciated realisation: as a leader, you are never not role-modelling. How you 'show up' every single day and apply yourself to the drive for excellence (or not) is noticed, more or less consciously, by everyone in your organisation. No pressure!

LEADING MY TEAM

- Set and maintain a standard of performance excellence and challenge members of your team who are falling into the trap of pursuing perfectionism.
- Ask members of your team periodically how you are doing. What are you doing effectively as leader? What could you be doing better? Where do you act or behave inconsistently with your words? Make a plan of how to improve when patterns and themes become clear in the feedback you are getting.

■ Challenge members of the team who fail to uphold the standards that the team have agreed to. Provide support to improve their performance whilst also insisting that standards improve within a specified timeline.

■ When goal-setting, encourage three levels to aim for: gold, silver and bronze standard, or similar. The gold standard would be a goal that would be achievable if everything went exactly to plan or better. Scale silver and bronze goals from there.

■ Review all goals when completed to see how much more you could have aimed for when setting them.

LEADING MY ORGANISATION

■ When you notice people in the wider organisation achieving goals, such as sales targets, in a way that is inconsistent with how the organisation expects people to behave, do something. Speak up. Challenge. Find a route to feedback your views.

■ Don't be afraid to discuss openly when peers are falling behind. Seek to understand why that might be and how you might be able to support them.

■ Play a role in organisational change initiatives early in the process. Become a leader who is recognised as adding value and enthusiasm to company wide change programmes. This sets you up as a progressive role-model.

■ Regularly seek feedback from your line manager (and other line managers if appropriate) about how you are doing. Don't wait for the mid-year or annual appraisal cycle. Express that you are keen to do the best job possible and ask that they hold you to the highest levels of performance.

DELIVER ON PROMISES

27. I deliver on promises and commitments made to others. Or put another way: do what you say you'll do.

People want to work for leaders who they can trust, whose perspective they value and who are open-minded. They also want to be led by someone who will do what they say they will do. In our experience, high performers like to be held to such standards too.

How do you feel about someone who says they will do something and they don't do it? How do you feel the next time they say they will deliver on a project and yet don't? You might give them a second or a third chance, but inevitably, in your eyes, their credibility gets eroded.

If you commit, ensure you follow through on delivery.

Here are a few reasons to sharpen your delivery focus:

1. **Integrity:** effective leaders value honesty. 'My word is my bond' encapsulates the idea of integrity in the workplace when it comes to delivery. Delivering what and when you promise to is not only really important for the perception others hold of you, but it is also important to how you view yourself. If you commit to something, be sure to deliver.

2. **Trust:** people hesitate to trust people who don't keep their word. If someone lets us down a number of times, then we tend to judge that they are unreliable and untrustworthy. A leader's relationships thrive on such trust, both with those they lead and with those they are ultimately answerable to – their own line manager, the board or shareholders.

3. **Credibility:** credibility is a reflection of our knowledge and experience. Credibility about ourselves is difficult to claim – despite the many self-proclaimed 'thought-leaders' on the web. It is for others to judge. The best we can do is influence the perceptions others have of us as a leader by building our credibility over time.

LEADING MY TEAM

- Make sure that a performance imperative for your team is that they are well prepared and know the detail. Nothing erodes trust in a team more than when people are exposed as being ill-prepared for a meeting, presentation or pitch.

- As a team, regularly review the timelines on projects to ensure milestones are achieved on (or before) the agreed dates. As a leader, you must insist your team share accurate details about progress here. Do not accept vague promises. Build a culture of honesty about progress and problems, so solutions can be found well ahead of time, if required.

- Without getting trapped in perfectionism, demand high quality of thinking and doing. Don't settle. This is not a change that you can bring about with your team overnight. If things have been a little lax to this point you need to introduce such shifts in expectations clearly and steadily. People will need lots of support from you early in such a transition.

LEADING MY ORGANISATION

- Lead project teams that are wider and more mixed than your own team and establish the same ways of working with a high delivery focus that you have built with your team.

- Seek opportunities to learn from outside your organisation. Is there a competitor or supplier who has a laser-like focus on delivering on their promises? Create an opportunity to learn from them and bring those insights back to your own organisation and develop new ways of working that will raise performance.

- Learn about two key approaches: agile and lean. Whilst these approaches originated in the manufacturing and engineering spheres, they are now widely employed as methodologies to enable many organisations to produce innovation quickly and efficiently. Becoming well-versed in these approaches will enable you to influence the way your organisation creates and delivers.

VALUES CHAMPION

28. I champion organisational values for others. Or put another way: values need to run through you like the words in a stick of rock.

'Are we living the values or just laminating them?' This is the classic question about the relevance of organisational values we were both asked early in our careers. Most organisations now do a great job in working up values statements for the business and publish them in creative and sometimes spectacular ways. They read brilliantly in the company brochure, website or in the lobby of head office. In the best cases, large groups of employees have had their say in defining them and identifying behaviours that would illustrate each value in action. Unfortunately, for all but the best leaders, this is seen as 'job done'.

The concept of values-based organisations and leadership has been around for some time. We need to look back to philosophers of the past for some context of values and their role in shaping human behaviour. Plato, Hobbes and Rousseau deliberated over the problems of social conscience, in a similar way that many of the organisations we work with do today. Most students of leadership would agree that the increased predictability of behaviour of people with similar values enhances collaboration between leaders and followers. Followers are more likely to thrive when values are aligned across a team or organisation.

Leaders understand that values are a highly individual thing. Thus, they become an ongoing discussion – a continuous checking and re-checking of what matters most to people. Indeed, research has proven that, whilst both clarity of organisational values and personal values are important, when it comes to commitment to work, gaining clarity of personal values has the most significant impact on engagement at work. Outstanding leadership relies on you understanding what is important to you and to each of the people that work for you.

LEADING MY TEAM

- Once you have gained clarity over the values that you hold and you think are important for the performance of your team, create time to share that with the team. Make sure people understand this is your set of values and that they do not need to hold the same things dear to them. NB: individuality is probably an important value to appear on your list.

- Depending on the relationship and state of your team, you may be able to create a safe environment, with no judgement or criticism, where your team can share their values with each other and you.

- Over time get to know the members of your team in some depth. This is not going to happen as a result of a single one-to-one meeting. Nor will it be the product of a solitary team away day. Notice what each person gets excited or frustrated about in their daily work. When are they at their best and why is that? Answers to such questions will provide you with clues about the values they hold.

LEADING MY ORGANISATION

- We would expect that your organisation has completed an exercise where it has generated some 'company values'. Do you know what they are? Do you know how you are expected to role-model these as a leader? It is less important that you can list them off than you know how to translate them into high-performing behaviours.

- Ensure that the values are mapped across to those of your own team. Explore with your team members how close they are and where there might be gaps. Agree how to proceed.

- Schedule a meeting with your function's human resources business partner or a member of the learning and development team. Ask them to share their thoughts on the organisation's values – even if there isn't a formal set yet – and your role as a leader in living these every day. Commit to acting in line with the outputs from this discussion.

INTEGRITY

29. I act with integrity. Or put another way: become the good corporate citizen.

Doing the right thing is always the right thing. The challenge is knowing what the right thing is in any given situation, especially when you have responsibility for a significant group of people and set of results. Being guided by your own integrity is key to making good decisions more consistently.

Integrity is a word open to interpretation. It covers aspects of character, honour, ethical and righteous behaviour. It speaks to the idea that a person's word is their bond and that when someone commits to doing something they will give of their best in order to achieve it. It is not always a guarantee of whether they succeed or not but that they did everything they could to deliver on their promise. Always.

When we talk about integrity, the result is less significant than the intention and the effort put into achieving the best outcome possible. If the intention was pure and you can evidence your rationale, you can still be said to have acted with integrity.

The clearer you are about your purpose and the values and beliefs you hold dear to you, the easier it is to maintain a sense of integrity. You may be asked to make a person redundant that you don't feel has been treated fairly by your organisation. What do you do? Well, ultimately, you may not prevent that person from being made redundant, but as a leader you would not let your feelings and thoughts about the situation go unheard, as that would clash with your own sense of fairness and what is deemed just.

You would speak up in such situations, make a case and try to influence at least a review of the situation – even when the business case for the decision is clear. The question that you can find that you ask yourself is: 'Is it right to let this slide without saying something?' or 'Am I ok with me not saying something about what feels wrong here?' Then you can tap into your own values to check the right course of action. Usually, you'll know when right is right.

LEADING MY TEAM

- Work with your team to co-create a set of guidelines about how you will make effective, ethical and fair business decisions. Ensure that these are agreed and clearly recorded.

- Check that your new guidelines fall within organisational frameworks such as any HR policies. There's no point in working outside of such things.

- Employ these guidelines, especially at critical points when there is no clear and obvious way forward. Let the 'rules' guide how you all decide which route to take.

- Where you use these guidelines, review how effective they were after each key decision. Decide if you need to add, subtract or change them in any way to make them an even better resource.

- When you have a particularly tricky decision to make, be sure to have someone that you can rely on for impartial advice who will act as a sounding board for you. A mentor, coach or peer can be a great source of such support.

LEADING MY ORGANISATION

- Reframe for yourself the role you have as a leader. Yes, you lead your team, but it is important you realise and accept that you are also an important resource for the wider organisation. Step up and take on the role of a leader who has the protection of the whole organisation as a key responsibility.

- Become an informal ambassador of doing the right thing. No need to act all authoritarian or purest about it. Equally, do not shy away from speaking up when you become aware that things are not being done as well as they might.

- Volunteer for project teams, special interest panels and strategy groups where you think you can add some value or where you are going to learn about how the organisation wants to produce great results. Has a diversity and inclusion group just been set up at work? Get on it. Is there a wellness working party starting soon? Volunteer to contribute.

HIGH PERFORMANCE

30. I build a culture of excellence and high performance. Or put another way: welcome to Accountability Central.

Accountability is a cornerstone of creating a culture of high performance for yourself, your team and organisation.

People who have high levels of accountability take personal and complete responsibility for producing a relevant, timely result that demonstrates excellence.

Let's dig into this idea a bit, as there are several important elements that make up the whole:

PERSONAL AND COMPLETE RESPONSIBILITY

Leaders who are high on accountability don't need to do all the work themselves but they tend to be comfortable taking the ultimate responsibility for delivery.

RELEVANT AND TIMELY RESULT

Leaders know that they cannot deliver all the results themselves and, as a result, do at least two things really well to ensure that results are delivered on time:

- First, they know who in their team has the right skills and can be trusted to deliver the result that is fit for purpose.
- Second, those same leaders also have excellent systems for monitoring the progress of current work streams. Rarely does a project slip out of their vision and get missed as a result. They avoid suffocating those who are charged with delivery but they also refuse to take a *laissez-faire* approach.

DEMONSTRATES EXCELLENCE

As a leader, set a standard of excellence that is known by all your team and organisation. Start by holding yourself to that standard. Then demand that of your team. You simply can't expect your team to excel if they are looking at you regularly failing to demonstrate high levels of accountability.

Building a culture of accountability produces several great outcomes for you, the team and your business because it does the following:

1. Reduces your time in motivating people to give of their best – they do that themselves.
2. Saves time on root cause analysis because people take control of their results and own up to mistakes.
3. Increases the time you have available to lead effectively, rather than get bogged down in the detail.
4. Becomes a self-selecting and de-selecting environment where you start to attract high performers and shed those that don't want to take accountability.
5. Enables high performance to become much more self-sustaining over the longer term.

LEADING MY TEAM

■ Set up a daily team meeting where progress is reviewed.

■ Ask each team member to report specifically on what they achieved yesterday. Ask people to commit to what they will deliver today.

■ Make sure that each comment is tracked – spreadsheets are good for this – so you know how every part of your team is progressing.

■ Provide a blend of some challenge and support. Mix this up depending on what you feel is likely to help someone improve their performance. For example, sometimes a supportive word or two or sometimes a more direct enquiry about why progress seems to have stalled.

■ Recognise achievement of team members when they deliver key milestones. Periodically adjust what people get recognition for to ensure the standard is being raised.

■ Ensure the team know what you are working on and the results you have produced. After all, you are a part of the team and this is a great way to build a culture where everyone is expected to perform at a high level all the time.

LEADING MY ORGANISATION

■ Prioritise leading your own performance. Ensure your track record is exemplary. Do great work in your technical area and in your role as leader.

■ Next, ensure your team is in the best place possible when it comes to performance and how others view it.

■ Support the performance of your peers. Review what each is involved in and offer support where you can.

■ Schedule a meeting with your line manager to share your insights into what is going well and what you are doing to drive performance to the next level. Ask for their input into anything you may have missed or could be doing differently.

■ In the right forum and in the right way, challenge where your peers and your boss could be doing things better. Now do you see why you and your team's performance needs to be awesome?

■ If you observe poor performance at any level of the organisation, step into your role as a leader within the organisation and challenge such unacceptable standards.

CHAPTER 9
ADVOCATES EXCELLENCE

AN INTRODUCTION TO ADVOCATING EXCELLENCE

Leaders describe a compelling picture of what the future could look like and appeal to others to share in future success. Speaking with clarity and confidence they generate commitment and enthusiasm for a shared vision or cause, and illustrate for others how their ambitions can be realised. They set high standards for people to live up to by painting pictures of what excellence looks like and encouraging others to work towards that picture.

THE FUTURE

> 31. I describe a captivating picture of what the future could look like. Or put another way: see your way to being a visionary.

Want to engage great people fully? Then you'll need to create a shared vision of excellence.

The clearer people are about what they are trying to achieve, the greater the likelihood that they will be able to perform at a consistently high level.

You will, doubtless, have heard that if you can dream it, you can do it. Probably not helpful advice to take too literally but it does align to the idea that visualisation is a key tool, employed by the highest performers in all sorts of fields from sport through acting to the military. 'Seeing' a future state builds a sense that something is achievable and provides a sense of certainty that otherwise would be missing. This sense of confidence, in turn, makes 'going for it' engaging, rather than frightening.

The richer the mental picture people can build, the better you and your team will be able to absorb and own the vision that you have created. The most effective visioning has even resulted in athletes increasing their physical strength during experiments without them even going into a gym.

Anita Roddick, inspirational founder and leader of the Body Shop International plc, declared that only you can see your vision. She makes a really important point: only you can see your vision as you see it and if you remain in a locked room and create the vision in isolation, your team will probably not get it. It will be something so unique to you that you will have difficulty sharing that effectively with others.

The key message here is to engage as many people as you can practically in the creation of your team's vision. Spend time on it. A vision is not something achieved on a team away day. It often takes many iterations and refinements. However, the clearer your purpose, the easier you will find creating your vision for what you are trying to achieve.

LEADING MY TEAM

- In your next one-to-one meeting with members of your team, ask what they think your team could or should be achieving.

- Gather all the responses together and identify any clear themes. Compare these themes to your own ideas for the future of your team and the team's purpose.

- Next, spend time with the team shaping a vivid picture of what the future shape of the team will be and what the key achievements should be.

- A helpful question to use here is, 'When we achieve our mission, what will this team be like in five or ten years' time?'

- It is useful to ensure you engage further with at least two people – one champion who loves the new version of the vision and one sceptic who is much less engaged. Work with them both together and separately until the vision is shaped to a place where both can 'see it'.

LEADING MY ORGANISATION

- It is likely that your organisation has already created a vision. Your first job as a leader is to get familiar with that vision and understand its implications in relation to your role as a leader.

- The organisation vision will either be explicit about, or infer, certain values and standards for leaders. Check your actions against the vision frequently.

- Ensure that the vision you create with your team, and the key objectives you set, are aligned with the wider organisation-level vision. The work your team is doing should be in service of the organisation achieving its vision.

- When your line manager sets you a project or objective to deliver, always check it against the wider vision. If you can't see a connection between your work and the organisation's vision, ask your boss about it. Make sure you can see direct connections.

- When your organisation creates a new vision, ensure people know you are keen to get involved. Really engage at the early stages if you can. This will give you a great insight into the strategic thinking of the organisation and help you align the work of your team more fully.

AMBITIONS

32. I illustrate to others how their own ambitions can be fulfilled. Or put another way: be able to respond to 'What's in it for me?'

Followers are unlikely to commit to your ideas and projects unless the connection to business results is clear and, importantly, they can see some benefit for themselves. It is quite simply human nature to ask questions in this way when being asked to join something that will be challenging and hard work. 'Why should I bring my discretionary effort to work in order to support your idea?'

Creating meaning requires that you understand the make-up of your audience in detail so that you can make connections and have an impact. When planning, excellent communicators work from their audience back to the message, whether they are planning for one person, three people or a hundred people. They research their audience as follows:

- What is on the mind of the audience right now?

- What is keeping them awake at night?

- What are their current challenges and how can what you want to say help them?

They design their communication so that in the early part of the conversation or presentation they are connecting in an area that matters to the listener, adapting their approach in order to embrace the audience's point of view.

Research tells us that you have not communicated well unless people:

- are clear on what you are saying
- accept that what you have to say is important
- feel concerned enough about the issue to want to do something about it
- have a clear idea of what it is they want or need to do as a result of your communication.

No matter how well you planned, you will need to learn to adapt your communications on your feet. Gather information constantly that could in any way be useful to you in building engagement. Learn about your audience's hot buttons in the moment and make adjustments to the message and your delivery.

LEADING MY TEAM

- Review the frequency of meetings you hold with each member of your team. Alter your diary to guarantee you meet with each person at least once a fortnight. Less frequently than that and you'll fail to be sufficiently up to date.

- Make the one-to-one meeting a chance to discuss their work but also create time explicitly to explore what is currently important for them, where their thinking is in relation to how the team is operating, how you are leading them and so on.

- In team meetings, ask your team to review their work against the purpose, vision and mission of the team. Regular check-ins about these key strategic team tools offers opportunities for each person to take ownership for keeping the team on track – a track that they were involved in designing.

LEADING MY ORGANISATION

- When you have an important presentation to make to your line manager or members of a senior team, plan the presentation in detail from the perspective of the audience first. Only then consider the content.

- Here are 10 helpful questions you can ask yourself to help raise your awareness of your audience. The answers will help you shape your content.

  1. Who is in the room?
  2. Why is each person present?

3. How might each person feel about the subject of your presentation?
4. What is in it for them if they do what you are asking them to do?
5. How do you make your message more appealing for each audience member?
6. How do you need to show up in order to influence effectively? How should you dress? What level of energy should you convey? What tone of voice?
7. How can you help each person to solve their problems?
8. Are you clear on what you want them to do?
9. How might they resist your message and how will you deal with this resistance?
10. What sticky moments or tricky questions do you anticipate and how will you respond?

HIGH STANDARDS

33. I set high standards for people to live up to, including myself. Or put another way: become the standard bearer.

Leaders are very good at setting clear standards, which they communicate clearly to the people they lead. If we went to speak to your team, how clear would they be about the standards you expect of them?

If you know your own purpose as a leader and you have worked with the team on identifying its purpose and the role of each individual within the team, then clarity about standards should not be a problem. The fuzzier you are about the purpose, vision and mission of the team, the more difficult it is for people to know what you expect. So, your first step in improving your leadership is making sure each member of your team has a clear sense of the team's purpose, vision and identity.

Once you have these strategic tools for your team in place, you can drill down into the detail of:

■ the results you expect people to produce
■ how you expect people to behave.

You and your whole team will benefit if everyone knows the specific details around these two key areas. Without being dictatorial about it, you should have a clear idea of what you perceive as excellence in the two key areas of performance and behaviour. Everyone will benefit further if deciding and codifying these into a 'Ways of working' document is a shared experience across the team.

Beware: don't mistakenly assume, as many leaders do initially, that because everyone has agreed standards, they will magically come to pass. No, they won't.

Highly excellence-focused teams need the leader to reinforce the consistency of the standards. This is mostly due to subtle differences in interpretation of what was meant by a particular standard, or simply that old habits can take a while to change. In a team setting, the leader acts as a guide and mentor to ensure consistency.

LEADING MY TEAM

■ From today, each and every time you set the team (or an individual) a key objective, be sure to get a commitment from them as to 'how' the result will be achieved, in addition to the details of 'what' success looks like. Outputs and behaviours must be aligned to the team purpose and vision.

■ Without micro-managing the work, regularly schedule in updates on progress.

■ Canvas members of the team, peers, customers and relevant others about *how* the project is progressing and feed comments back to the team or individual.

■ Recognise where great work is being done and challenge any areas that are not sufficiently close to the agreements made at the start of the process.

■ As great results get delivered, through discussion with your team develop a 'Ways of working' document that sets out how your team produces excellence. These principles will act as a guide and set the standard for future performance.

LEADING MY ORGANISATION

■ A minimum requirement is that your own track record of 'what' and 'how' you perform as a leader within the organisation is as good as you can make it.

■ Remember, we're not looking for perfection but building to excellence over time.

■ Review areas of your leadership that are currently not to the standard of excellence your organisation expects from you. Commit to making changes to up your game.

- Volunteer for project teams outside your area or take a particular area of burden from your line manager and set your own personal standard before starting. Commit to how you will 'show up' and the excellence in the work you will produce and hold yourself to such commitments.

- Where you see behaviour that is not ok, find a way to challenge it or report it. Certain things you can challenge in the moment, and that is sufficient, such as tittle-tattle at the water cooler. Other things that also need you to report on them include workplace bullying. Don't be afraid to hold others to a high standard too.

CLARITY AND CONFIDENCE

34. I speak with clarity and confidence in public forums. Or put another way: speak up! We can't hear you.

If you are not committed, somehow or other it will show through like a spotlight as you speak. People can smell passion and commitment and energy and determination – or the absence thereof.

Tom Peters

The best leaders have passion for their subject. If you want others to care as much as you do about your message, you need to express this. You will manage to express this with greater energy and clarity if you have a deep connection with the message. When what you say is really important to you, then you can communicate more naturally and confidently.

Before you can convince an audience to accept anything you say, they have to accept you as credible. Ask yourself:

- Do the people I am communicating with respect me?
- Do people feel that I am trustworthy?
- Does the audience believe I know what I'm talking about?

Critically, it isn't enough for you to know that you are living these principles – your audience needs to know this.

Our values are our beliefs in action. They are expressed through what we do, what we say and how we say it. Values make us believable in the eyes and ears of the listener. Research[i] on 'source credibility' tells us that in order to convince people we must be worthy of their trust and be competent at what we do every day.

Importantly, we need to couple this trust that others place in us with being dynamic and inspiring. People will respond to you if you share your passion for your subject – and they will see right through you if you pretend. Stand up for something that you truly believe in and you will find a way to connect.

LEADING MY TEAM

Whether you are communicating just to your team or a wider audience, here are tips for communicating like a professional:

- **Rehearse:** a great business speaker like Steve Jobs made things look effortless because of his obsession with rehearsal.

- **Practise without slides or script:** if you are going to talk to the audience, you will need to be able to speak without detailed notes.

- **Record yourself on video:** play it back and note where you could improve. In our experience, this is an underrated mode of practice and so easy to do now with mobile technology.

- **Rehearse in front of a trusted friend:** get them to give you some honest feedback on your conviction and clarity.

- **Rehearse responses:** work on answering tricky questions that you anticipate being asked. Use your values as a guide.

- **Ask for feedback:** after a 'live' piece of communication, invite feedback on your performance from members of the audience.

Communicating as effectively as you can, also set a standard for members of your team when it is time for them to take the spotlight.

LEADING MY ORGANISATION

- Commit to developing into a really effective public speaker. As we have shown, it is a vital skill set for you as a leader. Moreover, becoming recognised as a great speaker will result in you being asked to do more public speaking, which in turn raises your profile as a leader within and beyond your organisation.

- Look for opportunities outside your organisation to speak in public. Start small and in an area in which you are confident of your knowledge. It may be that you start by finding speaking occasions where you could talk about a passion of yours that is not work-related. Go and speak to pupils at your local school or chamber of commerce. Any chance to develop this skill should be taken. Take a deep breath and go for it!

COMMITMENT

35. I demonstrate excitement and commitment to the vision. Or put another way: we're all buzzing now.

Is it a good thing to build a work culture and environment where there is a sense of excitement? Is work the appropriate place to have a constant buzz that is generated by the leader and perpetuated by the rest? Let's see.

We guess that, like many of you, we were raised to respect authority – unquestioningly. We were also encouraged to view work as a place where serious endeavour and application were rewarded. Yes, we know: well-intentioned but naïve!

Much of this hard work ethic was helpful, of course. However, the thing it prompted as a by-product was that it proved hard to do anything other than find work an incredibly serious place. In our early careers – albeit in quite different spheres – we were always careful not to be seen to be enjoying our time too much because we were surrounded by leaders and managers who viewed work similarly to the way we did: all work and no play.

But there is a serious flaw in the way leaders are thinking if deadly serious is the over-riding organisational tone. It assumes that a serious environment reflects, or at least produces, a committed attitude. It doesn't necessarily. It is worth recalling here that correlation is not the same as causation.

On the flip side, too much whooping and hollering doesn't work too well either. After hundreds of meetings with leaders over the last 17 years, we are convinced that 'fluff' doesn't cut it. All noise and no substance is certainly not leadership. At best it's cheerleading and at worst it's inefficient and patronising.

However, it is also certain that a sterile environment that fails to seize opportunities for building genuine excitement about whatever is trying to be achieved is not effective leadership either. At best it's controlling. At worst it fails to maximise the parts of being human that excel and produce incredible results when energised to do so. The best leaders understand the need for such well-balanced enthusiasm and create ways to generate it, especially at key times and on important projects.

LEADING MY TEAM

- Develop a sense of the mood of your team. Is the energy high and engaged at the moment? Is there a quiet sense of determination and effort? Are people exhausted and lacklustre? These are all sensitivities it will be useful for you to learn.

- It behoves you to be aware of your own mood and energy and how that might be impacting the team. A leader's temperament is infectious, so be acutely aware of what you are projecting.

- Check in with each of your direct reports regularly to see how they are feeling. This helps you to assist them early if the need arises, or challenge where appropriate.

- Just varying how you do routine tasks can provide the little injection of energy that is required. The list of possibilities is endless but includes:

  - holding a team meeting at a different time or location
  - accompanying a team member on a customer visit
  - attending a conference with a couple of the team.

LEADING MY ORGANISATION

- Commit that whenever you are outside of your team setting that you will be an ambassador for it. Represent the team with energy and commitment to the greater good.

- Where you can, inspire others to up their game. When you have developed a good relationship with peers and more senior leaders, hustle them along a little if you notice they don't seem to be giving everything required to perform at the highest level.

- Offer to act as a mentor within the organisation. Be keen to help other junior leaders develop and make sure you role-model excellent behaviours when undertaking this important role. *Note*: if you can't bring your best self to such a role, please don't offer.

- Seek opportunities to share the vision of your team with others. This will set you apart as a leader who is driven to deliver great performance for the benefit of your team members, customers and the wider organisation.

CHAPTER 10
APPRECIATES EXCELLENCE

AN INTRODUCTION TO APPRECIATING EXCELLENCE

Leaders ensure that people are rewarded for work that delivers results and they recognise people who live up to shared values. Always looking to challenge their own thinking and assumptions, they embrace multiple perspectives. They encourage innovative thinking and constantly seek to generate the small improvements in performance that make the biggest impact. They look outside the organisational boundaries for inspiration and new thinking. Creating an environment in which people feel valued for speaking honestly and encouraged to share ideas and beliefs is important to them.

RECOGNITION

36. I make sure that people are recognised for work that delivers results. Or put another way: have you ever had *too much* recognition?

Have you ever had too much recognition? Unlikely. We have asked hundreds of people this question over the years and no one has yet answered 'Yes!' We get into plenty of hypothetical arguments with people around how recognition can be over-done, yet not one person that we have spoken to can point to an example of them having been the victim of over-recognition. They will talk about examples of where it could have been done more effectively or where it didn't go well at all. Most often, though, the bigger concern is that people really struggle to even identify one significant example of recognition from their entire career.

The truth is we are all more vulnerable and needy than we like to imagine. What is more, appreciating the great work of others will make you feel better about yourself. It will also increase the likelihood that your followers will invest more in their work – and in you.

In the workplace, researchers such as Barbara Fredrickson have found that, amongst high-performing teams, the expression of positive feedback outweighs that of negative feedback by a ratio of 5.6 to 1. By contrast, low-performing teams have a ratio of 0.36 to 1.

Recognition = confirms that people and the work matters.

To be clear, we are not talking about recognition for showing up at work each day. We are talking about recognition to highlight what great work looks like for the recipient and for others watching on. We are talking about the kind of recognition that:

- acknowledges people's value to the business
- makes people feel better about our work and want to repeat the success
- fuels people's motivation
- when public, has the effect of showing other people what matters and what counts, setting the example to others and communicating the standard of performance you are looking for
- promotes excellence.

LEADING MY TEAM

- Pay attention to what is happening around you.
- Look out and listen out for the exceptional and never walk past an opportunity to reinforce what counts.
- Be clear about what deserves recognition. *Hint*: this will, almost always, be about the 'what and how' of performance in service of achieving the team vision.
- Understand your own preferences in relation to recognising others, but, more importantly, be clear about how others prefer to be recognised.
- If you are one to brush off compliments, consider that a compliment may well have been directed at you but it is also a recognition of the work of your team. Don't be so quick to dismiss it, even if it doesn't mean that much to your own performance.
- Review regularly how the recognition you are giving has an impact on performance and adjust accordingly – which usually means do more, rather than less.

LEADING MY ORGANISATION

■ Give people in your team plenty of recognition beyond the team. Make sure your line manager is aware of the excellent work that members of your team are delivering. Don't be shy or too matter of fact about exceptional performance. If you don't raise awareness of it, nobody else is likely to.

■ Recognise people from beyond your team in appropriate public forums. Being keen to ensure others are noticed for doing great work role-models a willingness to appreciate excellence wherever you see it as a leader.

■ Challenge organisational cultures that do not recognise excellence sufficiently. Be clear that you are not necessarily raising the issue of financial reward, but one where all senior leaders adequately appreciate the exceptional work that many individuals contribute to the wider organisational aspirations. Become a champion of recognition.

INNOVATIVE THINKING

37. I embrace different perspectives and encourage innovative thinking. Or put another way: tell-tale signs your team is in trouble and what you can do about it.

Earlier, we painted a picture of the ever-increasing pace of change under which organisations are operating. There are three tell-tale signs that your team is not best placed to operate effectively in this new world:

■ People are holding on to the old ways of doing things.

■ People are resisting the new ways of doing things.

■ People lack the creativity, confidence or time to innovate.

'When Sue was here, we ...'

If you hear people refer to the way things were in the past, there is an underlying desire to hold on to the certainty that came from knowing how things were done. There was little effort required to work in a way that had become familiar and routine.

As a leader, if you hear this sort of commentary, then you need to do two things. First, acknowledge the success of past achievements whilst explaining why the old ways of working are no longer fit for purpose. But, second, don't throw out the baby with the bathwater. Hold on to what still works wherever you can, as that will honour previous work and help people make the transition.

'We've always done it that way.'

A close cousin of the first phrase, this feels different. Whilst it is a reference to the past, it seems more resistant to a new way of doing things. It also suggests just one way of doing things. High-quality teams have a tendency to be constantly looking for better ways of doing things – even when performance is strong.

'Hey boss, can I just check something with you?'

Look around your desk or workstation. Is there literally, or metaphorically, a well-worn path to your desk? If so, it suggests that your team members are not thinking for themselves. The team look to you for their solutions too often. They are using you as the least line of resistance to create answers to problems. Even those that come to you with an idea are still looking for something from you – confirmation.

LEADING MY TEAM

- Ask questions to promote thinking and creativity.
- Use the supportive nature of a coaching style in combination with high challenge so your people realise quickly that avoiding taking ownership for creating appropriate solutions for challenges is not ok.
- Reinforce innovative work by recognising it at appropriate times as publicly as feels right.
- Push people to create a range of solutions that include some that are at the more extreme end of realistic. Encourage this 'big thinking' to generate greater innovation.
- Create a working group that keeps up to date with new developments in your technical area. Ask the group to feed back monthly to the wider team what they have discovered and make recommendations of how to incorporate findings into how the team operates.
- Create opportunities for members of your team to get experience from other parts of the business or even other industries. Agree the focus of any such opportunity and ensure they bring back what they have learned and apply it to your team setting.

LEADING MY ORGANISATION

- Ask your line manager or learning and development team about business exchange programmes and take an opportunity for a short-term secondment. These are great ways to add value back to your organisation through your widened experience.

- Similarly, pursue an advanced qualification or degree in your technical area or in leadership. Be clear about the benefits to the organisation and deliver on this as part of the commitment.

- Listen intently to and appreciate different views of peers and your own manager. Importantly, try to understand why it is that they may hold a different view about things than you do. Ask yourself regularly, 'What if I was wrong?'

- When in a meeting or project team, be the person who pushes for greater innovation and creativity. Position yourself as the activist for change and improvement.

PROGRESS

38. I constantly seek to generate small improvements in performance that represent progress. Or put another way: all those 1% improvements add up.

Leaders know that it is their job to facilitate progress in the work that their people care deeply about. The concept of generating small improvements in organisations can be traced back to Toyota and Kaizen – a philosophy of working that suggests no business process is ever fully optimised and that there is always room for improvement. Also known as:

- marginal gains
- 1 per cent-ers
- critical non-essentials
- small wins.

This more popular language describing, essentially, the same principle has emerged through sports leaders such as Sir Clive Woodward and Sir Dave Brailsford. These guys are never satisfied. They lie awake at night asking themselves:

- What could make this even better?
- What else?
- What next?
- And then what?

They create the conditions in the organisation that ensure others are equally critical of current practice and are not shy of setting up the discussions that are at the centre of progress.

However, progress in itself is not sufficient to fuel motivation and performance. It is the leader's job not only to ensure that progress occurs, but also to acknowledge that it has occurred, that the benefits are felt and those involved are publicly recognised. People are motivated internally by doing work that leads to small wins but are not always great at spotting them when they occur: 'I was just doing my job.' People want to hear from you that they are doing work that is meaningful and purposeful – this nourishes and provides essential motivation, particularly in tough times.

Importantly, when your team members have been involved in conversations or activities that deliver progress – something that is meaningful and connects to the higher order purpose of the team – they are more likely to be open to taking the next step in the project, no matter how daunting and challenging it may appear. They are more likely to want to be involved in, and contribute to, processes and conversations designed to overcome vexing problems and discover creative solutions.

LEADING MY TEAM

Here's how you can begin to make consistent improvement, a part of how you lead your team:

- **Organise a review group:** include people from a wide range of disciplines and invite people who have a variety of different thinking styles. Appoint one person to record the ideas that come from each session.

- **Clarify the problem:** clearly define the problem that you want to solve and the gap you're looking to close between the current and desired state. Make it clear that the purpose of the session is to generate as many ideas as possible.

- **Share ideas:** when everyone has shared their ideas, start a group discussion to develop each idea further, and use them to create new ideas. Building on other people's ideas is one of the most valuable aspects of group brainstorming.

- **Review:** sort through these ideas to find the best. Use your judgement to choose the best ideas to try. Commit to how and when with review timescales too.

- **Make it fun!**

LEADING MY ORGANISATION

- Constantly be asking in forums outside of your team:
  - Is this process or approach still fit for purpose?
  - How could we do this better?
  - How would the best organisation in the world approach this?
  - And other such provocative questions to prompt a drive for excellence.
- When you have a key project to deliver, ask your line manager for advice on your suggested approach. Ask them to suggest alternative ways to improve on your options based on their experience and expertise. Even if their offering doesn't provide an ideal solution, their input may well provide you with triggers to new thinking.
- As a leader of the organisation, engage in the dialogue where large-scale changes are proposed. Ask how you can help. Offer an alternative view. Challenge some assumptions. That is, after all, the role you have as a leader within the organisation.

LOOKING OUTSIDE

39. I look outside my team for inspiration and new thinking. Or put another way: we don't have all the answers.

We love working with leaders and teams that have the confidence in their ideas and the willingness to put them into action and to learn from successes and failures alike. When this approach is over-cooked, however, performance never quite reaches its full potential because:

- too much time is spent reinventing the wheel
- thinking becomes stale
- fresh perspectives and new possibilities fail to be seen.

Brilliant leaders use their network for a novel purpose: introducing new thinking from other spheres. Where a connection of theirs has already tackled an issue, they are quick to pick up the phone and arrange a meeting to learn about how it was successfully resolved. They are willing to step out into the unknown. They remain open to receiving ideas from anyone and anywhere. They spot good ideas and are willing to challenge the system to get new products, processes, services and systems adopted.

Working with the same team in the same way within the same organisation can lead to stale thinking. Approaches that remain similar over time lead to similar advantages and limitations to creativity. This is one reason that organisations that work in matrices rather than silos prove to be more innovative. Project teams are constantly changing and fresh thinking emerges.

Creativity is about generating unique solutions to problems in a way that adds value to the organisation. Leaders know that creativity is impossible without appropriate stimuli. They know that their potential to take the business forward is directly linked to their preparedness to explore and take on new perspectives. They know they don't have to have all the answers – they just need the energy to gather and process new thinking.

LEADING MY TEAM

Here are some approaches we see leaders encouraging their teams to adopt to fuel creativity:

- A widely read leader is more likely to be creative and able to inspire new thinking. Whilst it is clearly good that they read books, magazines and blogs that are outside what they would usually digest, it multiplies the benefits if they can encourage all team members to do the same.

- Urge your team to network broadly. Get them to hang out with some different people and obtain new perspectives on work.

- Insist all senior members of your team call customers and ask them for their views on current issues and your products or service.

- Hold walking meetings with individuals. Get outside when the weather allows and hold team meetings inspired by the local environment.

- Adopt a team charity that encourages you all to go and build or share skills with the charity or the beneficiaries to the work of the charity. Such experiences can be truly transformational in the way people look at business challenges.

LEADING MY ORGANISATION

- Share successes from your team as case studies when they have used particularly innovative ways to resolve key issues.

- Let peers know that you would welcome the opportunity to offer secondments to your team or exchanges with them for one of your talented team. Urge a sharing of expertise and thinking.

■ Build your network within and beyond your organisation and tap into it when you need a fresh perspective to benefit your team or the organisation.

■ Ask HR to source you a mentor who can develop your thinking as a leader. Insist that the mentor has an outstanding leadership record but that they come from outside your industry. If this works well, both you and the organisation can benefit hugely.

■ Encourage prototyping in project teams. It is an approach that accelerates the problem-solving process when time is short. It is about taking action quickly and learning from that action. It feeds our curiosity about what works and what doesn't work and can be almost playful in nature.

SHARE IDEAS

40. I create an environment in which people feel valued for speaking honestly and are encouraged to share ideas and beliefs. Or put another way: feel the fear ...

Openness, honesty, new ideas and fresh thinking are the heartbeat of excellence in organisations. Most of the leaders we have worked with over the years have claimed to want their followers to share what is on their mind, come to them with new ideas, express concerns openly, provide feedback on the leadership they experience and communicate potential problems early.

In coaching sessions, these leaders will say that they openly encourage this behaviour and regularly repeat the importance of sharing in this way at meetings with their team. Some leaders find their invitation has the desired effect. Others continue to be frustrated by the lack of communication and idea generation. As a result, they get only a false sense of what is really going on around them and little in terms of innovation.

Fear in your environment will mean your people will avoid risk. Instead, they will look to repeat what's worked for them in the past, take the safe option and don't rock the boat. Most leaders would like to see innovation and growth through change, yet allow fear to exist within their culture – mostly unwittingly.

Leaders know that they need to be alert to the signs that fear is in the system and take action to remove it. They know it takes time and effort but the reward for such effort could be the difference between success and failure. They also know that any change starts with them and how they treat people every day.

If you're not making mistakes, then you're not doing anything.

John Wooden

When people do speak up and talk about mistakes or problems, brilliant leaders listen, acknowledge they hear what was said and collect the real facts before making judgements. When the natural instinct is to respond too quickly and overreact, they manage fear by being patient and understanding.

LEADING MY TEAM

- Establish a team culture where there is a clearly understood and deeply held belief that mistakes are not failures – they are simply the process of eliminating ways that won't work in order to come closer to the ways that will.

- When mistakes occur, rather than getting upset and reprimanding people, first look in the mirror and determine what your role has been in the failure.

- Ask yourself regularly: are my expectations clear?

- When you fail to perform well or don't deliver, be quick to admit it. Role-model your fallible side. Ensure you share what you learned from the experience.

- When you get a sense that people are not being fully open and honest ask, 'What's really going on here?' This is a really powerful question to elicit feelings – especially fear – that may be being repressed.

- Set a ground rule for meetings that people not only can, but are required to, share thoughts and feelings openly in order that they can be tackled jointly.

LEADING MY ORGANISATION

- Speak up in meetings with your line manager and peers, rather than sit on things that need to be said. Failing to speak up honestly perpetuates situations that are less than ideal.

- If you get access to your organisation's most senior leaders, be keen to share your views and concerns. Make sure you do it with class – don't point the finger, don't stalk them and avoid using the wrong opportunity to share such concerns. Your raising of such issues at an annual awards evening may not be best appreciated. Ask for some time to share the observations you have.

- Keep your own line manager in the loop if you do want to air and share concerns at higher levels within the organisation. They won't appreciate not knowing what you are going to do as they could be exposed as not knowing what members of their team are doing.

CHAPTER 11
DEVELOPS EXCELLENCE

AN INTRODUCTION TO DEVELOPING EXCELLENCE

Great leaders are focused on increasing other people's belief in their ability and see it as a priority to help others raise their performance. People feel powerful and supported around them. However, they balance this with an open and honest communication style that encourages performance-focused feedback and challenges people to get better and better at what they do.

EMPATHY AND TRUST

41. I build strong relationships through empathy and trust. Or put another way: are you investing in relationships?

People will trust you, be they client, colleague or employee, to the extent that they know what your values are, and to the extent that they know you can be relied on to act in accordance with your values. If people don't know what your values are, they will not trust you and will not follow you. The more you are trusted by your colleagues, the more you will get from them and the more your team will thrive.

Beware: trust is as fragile as it is valuable. Lose it once and some people are not keen to extend it to you again in quite the same way. You can guard against this if you know what elements go to increasing trust. Understanding the elements of trust enables you to build these and make sure you do not destroy them. Trust sits at the cornerstone of all leadership relationships.

Leaders know that the element that has the largest single effect on the degree of trust someone will place in them is their orientation towards others. People need to be sure that you are clearly working for the greater good, for the team or the other person's benefit before your own. This is not to say that you will not have an agenda to achieve. It is just that, if someone feels you are out *only* for what you can get, you will undermine any other efforts to build trust and empathy. The more people sense leaders are genuinely interested in them and helping them to explore avenues of improvement, the more trust is built.

If people feel that you have let them down, the assumption might be that you were not focused on them sufficiently and that your attention was too firmly focused on what you felt was important to you. Failing to do what you said you were going to do when you said you were is often interpreted as a huge dose of self-orientation.

LEADING MY TEAM

- Really take time to get to know your team and what is important to them – professionally for sure, and personally, when the time and setting is right to do so.

- Work alongside members of your team whenever a situation presents itself where you can add some value. Be seen to be keen to help without getting dragged into micro-managing or doing work you don't need to do.

- Avoid over-promising. People prefer an over-achiever to an over-promiser.

- When you are given privileged information, retain the confidentiality that has been placed in you.

- Consider what projects and tasks to delegate to your team members based on their aspirations.

- Additionally, be aware of how people are at any given time and perhaps take a decision not to delegate something to them because of current workload or personal challenges.

LEADING MY ORGANISATION

- Take potential solutions to your line manager, rather than problems, wherever you can. Do the heavy lifting of the thinking before presenting issues to them.

- On occasion, when you know your own line manager is overwhelmed, consider not troubling them with your challenges until things calm down.

■ Go one step further and offer to take away anything from your boss that they might find useful to be relieved of. Sometimes, like you, they will get so into the current situation that they'll simply forget to ask for help and try to spin all plates all the time. You can be a great help in such situations.

■ Reflect on how your peers present ideas and make decisions. Next time it would be useful to get their help or influence them to take an action, position it being mindful of the perspectives they tend to take, as you'll find this approach far more effective.

FEEDBACK

42. I provide and encourage performance-focused feedback. Or put another way: how can we get better at what we do?

Great leaders develop the ability to accurately reflect on their own performance at work, identifying areas of strength that they could build on and gaps that they need to address. However, they are also never shy of asking others to provide feedback on how they could get better.

You may be aware of what is going on for you, but you can only judge how you are 'being' for other people by asking them. Asking others what they appreciate about you, and what you could do differently to be even more effective, is the only way to develop true self-awareness.

Lord Sebastian Coe, former Olympic Gold medal athlete, goes even further with his illustration of the importance of feedback in building a culture of high performance:

If you know something that will help me to get better at what I do –
and you are not telling me – you are letting me down.

Simply, if you want to encourage feedback within your team, then you need to be a great model for it, both giving and receiving.

And remember, when you ask for feedback, make sure you accept it in the spirit in which it is being offered – to make things or you better. Be open and grateful for their time and input, no matter what you learn about yourself.

What of those who have been asked to provide feedback? What should be their guiding principles? Quite simply, if you are looking to help people to want to grow and improve, do the following:

■ Make your feedback constructive, using it to positively reinforce good performance and highlight areas for improvement.

- Provide specific information and examples to back up your comments.
- Base your remarks on personal observations rather than hearsay.

Above all, set aside personal feelings of like or dislike in order to provide fair and balanced commentaries. This will genuinely open up opportunities for personal development.

LEADING MY TEAM

- Explain to your team the role of feedback in building a high-performance culture.

- Explore together how the team fares currently in terms of providing high quality to each other, from you and to you and stakeholders outside the team. Seek to understand why things are as they are.

- Commit over the long term to create a culture of high-performance feedback – avoid making this a big thing for a couple of weeks and then sliding backwards.

- Ask team members in your one-to-one conversations:
  - How am I doing?
  - What do I need to do more/less?
  - What can I do differently to bring out the best in you?

- Build performance feedback into project plans both at the completion of the project and, importantly, on an ongoing basis. Make sure people act on feedback.

LEADING MY ORGANISATION

- Whenever you are asked to contribute to 360° reports for other people, whether your team, peers or your line manager, consider it an honour and give it the due time, care and attention it deserves.

- Ask your own line manager and peers for feedback on your performance on a regular basis. This is a bit of a balance as 'regular basis' can soon turn into 'all the time' and become a bit of a burden to others, so judge this carefully. As long as you have sufficient data to keep making improvement, then enough is enough.

- Seek a mentor from within your organisation. Contract with them to provide you with some feedback on actually observed performance. Invite them to attend your team meetings and other important events and to discuss their views on your accomplishment.

COACH

43. I treat people as individuals and coach them towards excellence. Or put another way: there are no cookie-cutters here!

Effective leaders employ different styles to suit the situation. Their approach is dictated by a number of factors. Over time, leaders add styles that enable them to choose the best approach for each situation and each person. Leader-as-coach is one such style that works in several settings and can be added to your existing toolkit.

Here are three key tips to adopting a coaching approach into your management styles:

1. **Not in every situation.** There are a few situations when coaching is probably unhelpful. If there is immediate risk (personal, physical or reputational), a clear, well-communicated and directive approach probably works better. But there are plenty of opportunities when you can use a coaching approach:

   - performance reviews
   - project management challenges
   - attaining specific KPIs
   - career discussions.

   All the above and more benefit from you asking great questions and paying attention to the answers you get.

2. **Not with everyone.** It can be a challenge to coach upwards – to your boss. The culture of coaching within an organisation needs to be well established before it is easy to manage upwards this way.

   Additionally, some people just don't want to be coached at that moment. We're just being pragmatic in acknowledging that at times people just want the solution. Coaching is demanding for both parties: if someone is too tired to engage, they may just be happy for you to tell them the answer and occasionally we think that's ok.

3. **Not if you remain unconvinced.** There will be little worse for your team, your organisation and perhaps yourself than engaging in coaching without full commitment. You can't do it well without bringing your whole self to each coaching conversation.

Our advice: try a 'little and often' approach. No need to book a meeting room for two hours and attempt a full-on coaching session. You aren't a coach. You are a leader who uses a coaching style. Look for opportunities to engage in coaching conversations in real time, such as at the water cooler, on the walk to lunch and so on

Ask.

Pay attention to the reply.

Repeat.

Keep it simple and build on your successes and, above all, make it work for you. There is no 'one way' to coach effectively, so just have a go and enjoy the results.

LEADING MY TEAM

■ Establish with your team that you will be experimenting with a coaching style and that they can expect you to be asking more than you are telling.

■ Look for every opportunity within a conversation with your team members to employ some of the techniques of coaching: deep listening, a curious mindset and open-ended questions that encourage the recipients to think for themselves.

■ Keep your coaching interventions as conversational in style as you can. This is not a process as much as an entire way of demonstrating your leadership.

■ When you receive a response, dig a little deeper when it seems that you can encourage further reflection and learning.

■ If, ok, when things don't quite go to plan, as will happen from time to time, do what effective coaches do and look at what your role in that outcome was and ask: what could I have done differently? How did I influence the answers that I was given? How much leading or bias did I present in the questions I asked? What will I do differently next time?

LEADING MY ORGANISATION

■ Share your coaching aspirations with your peers and line manager and explain you are developing this new style to your leadership identity.

■ Find someone who is equally interested in exploring the practices of 'leader-as-coach', commit to working together to get better and provide each other with some coaching, as required.

■ Ask your line manager if you can pursue some coaching development opportunities that you can bring back to the team.

- Ask the learning and development department or HR if you can receive some coaching. There is no better way to learn how to coach well than by receiving effective coaching yourself. Both of us still receive coaching formally from other people so we can continue to develop.

- Offer to coach a junior member of staff from outside your team. They gain some free coaching whilst you get the chance to practise your skills. As a by-product the organisation wins too.

EXPLOIT STRENGTHS

44. I encourage people to exploit their strengths and manage their weaknesses. Or put another way: hire talented people and ask them to do what they do best.

Understanding what one is good for and what one therefore should try to strengthen and develop is key to self-development.

Peter Drucker

Creating a positive work environment begins by helping people focus on what they do best. In a recent UK poll conducted by The Skills Commission, one in five people questioned said they were in a job that that did not make best use of their skills, and 41% of people said they had been in that situation previously.

In an investigation into what 'employees want from the workplace', TalentSmoothie gathered data online from 2,521 survey participants. Their key findings included the following:

- A job that uses their strengths and includes personal development is seen as essential.

- Being allowed to use their strengths and being trusted were cited as their best experiences at work.

- Strengths-based recruitment matters.

The strengths approach starts with looking at what works and how an individual, team or business can build on this. This distinguishes the methodology from more traditional approaches to talent development that start with deficit, fixing problems or closing gaps.

Each person has a unique combination of core skills, abilities, qualities and traits that they enjoy using and can use easily. Focusing on success, what people and organisations are good at and where they have natural strengths makes sense. Focusing on success and maximising potential is recognised as the path to growth.

A positive approach does not ignore critical flaws, problems and challenges. It simply starts the conversation in a different place, which taps into people's passions, energy and interests, that in turn fuels drive and confidence. Through focusing on their own strengths, and the strengths of others in their team, people demonstrate a more positive attitude.

Most people understand their weaknesses far better than they do their strengths, and yet it is people's unique, personal qualities that provide energy and fuel performance. They highlight the road to mastery, confidence and achievement. It is the leader's role to help their people understand what they are good at and help people to make the best possible contribution to the organisation's goals.

LEADING MY TEAM

■ Check that you start to review the performance of individuals through a strengths-based lens first and foremost.

■ Don't ignore critical weaknesses but seek to help people leverage their strengths to address these.

■ The better you know the performance of your team and review it regularly, the better you will get to know their individual – and the team-level – strengths.

■ Ask each of the team to take a strengths profile, such as Gallup Strengths-Finder or our very own Leader iD diagnostic, to help them appreciate the strengths they have. Discuss the results in a one-to-one conversation using a coaching approach.

■ Share your own results from the Leader iD diagnostic to start the process of understanding and developing a strengths-based team culture.

■ As part of an annual appraisal cycle, share evidence you have for the strengths each team member possesses (see Appendix). Discuss how accurate your observations have been and plan together how to use them to raise team performance. Encourage each team member to volunteer specifically for roles or tasks that maximise their strengths.

LEADING MY ORGANISATION

■ Encourage peers within and beyond the organisation you work for to take a strengths-based profile such as the Leader iD diagnostic. Volunteer to chat about their results and to share your own in the spirit of seeking to improve.

- Discuss your strengths as you see them with your line manager. Check for harmony and dissonance.

- Seek a mentor who possesses great strengths in the areas that you would like to develop further and ask them to help you get better. Don't forget these could be strengths you want to make stronger or weaknesses you want to minimise.

- Offer to mentor others in areas where you are strong.

- Design project teams to have the right blend of strengths that will be required on the project. High customer focus? Ensure there are plenty on the team with strengths in compassion, discovery and balance.

RAISE THEIR GAME

45. I take personal responsibility for helping others to raise their performance. Or put another way: if you are not helping others raise their performance, then what are you spending your time doing?

Great leaders take it upon themselves to help the people in their team to raise their performance continuously. Sounds like common sense? Yes, but in our experience, not common practice. Too often we find ourselves working with leaders who believe that growing people is the responsibility of the human resources department. When this thinking is challenged, the barriers appear to be that people just don't see it as their job – they just don't have time for it even if they were minded to act. Performance reviews are simply a process driven by HR and a 60% completion rate is often seen as an acceptable result.

One study we looked at suggested that 62% of millennials have felt 'blindsided' by their performance reviews and 74% said they feel 'in the dark' about how their managers and peers think they're performing.

The most effective leaders we see make it their business to help others raise their game and see review conversations as a central part in this process. They invest in review conversations that:

- fuel performance (motivate)

- align work projects to business strategy (goals)

- identify the top performers to enable promotion and compensation (reward)

- target development activity (promote a growth mindset)

... and they engage in such conversations with a high degree of frequency.

The business of leaders at all levels is to help those in their charge develop beyond their dreams ... which in turn leads to happy customers, stakeholders and communities.

Tom Peters

Leaders make it their job to help their people:

■ become stronger, more confident contributors to the business goals

■ develop as human beings and leaders themselves

■ develop to become more valuable team members than when they first experienced your leadership.

The leader who sees their role as serving others, recognises the tremendous responsibility to do everything in their power to nurture the personal and professional growth of employees and colleagues.

LEADING MY TEAM

■ Accept as part of your core identity as a leader that an important role is to develop those in your team and beyond.

■ In every conversation you have with someone in your team, use the following powerful question to help you remain focused on supporting and developing them: 'What is my role in this conversation, with this person, at this time?' This self-directed question has worked very powerfully with hundreds of leaders who now practise it regularly.

■ Asking people in your team about their level of confidence to tackle a task or deliver a stretching target can be very liberating and reassuring for them and will also tell you as the leader a lot about their current capability. Take responses to this seriously and seek to support and develop where you can.

■ Regularly reviewing both outstanding performances and less successful efforts is key to driving high performance across the team. Neglect to do this regularly and you waste rich learning opportunities.

LEADING MY ORGANISATION

■ Support the work and development of your peers. This is not a zero-sum game: helping others will not mean you do less well. It is not a case of if they gain one step on a ladder you have to go back one step. You both win.

■ Offering your services as a mentor or coach to people beyond your team is a great way to add value to your organisation and a sign of highly developed leadership.

■ Challenge under-performance wherever you observe it, then follow that up with offers of support to help make things better than they were.

■ Continue to invest in developing yourself in service of others – become an increasingly good leader in order to add ever-more worthwhile value back to the organisation.

■ Whenever you are asked to contribute feedback on the performance of someone else, resist the temptation to ignore it or rush your input. If you are committed to developing others, then see these opportunities as the time to provide your most considered reflections and insights. That's what great leaders do, even when they could use the excuse of being too busy.

PART 4

LEADER iD PRACTICE PLANNING

CHAPTER 12
THREE TOOLS

YOUR COMMITMENT TO PRACTISE

So, it's a good idea now to review all your work from your Leader iD profile and the ideas you have collected from the 45 insights and make some plans. This is where the 'rubber hits the road'. You need to be honest with yourself and be in a position to answer the following question: what are you actually committing to practise as a result of your time invested in reading this book?

Three things separate those who are serious about their development from the 'also-rans':

■ a commitment to focused practice

■ a regular review of that practice

■ daily and weekly reflection of performance and personal growth.

This is your opportunity to identify what to practise and how. Then you'll need to commit to stepping back to review progress and accurately evaluate the impact of this practice on your followers, yourself and your results.

Taking action:
Doing what needs to be done
When it needs to done
In response to the needs of the situation.

Gregg Krech

Before you begin any detailed planning, take a few minutes to remind yourself of the following from the prompts offered throughout the book, such as:

■ your reflections on your scores from the Leader iD profile

■ your picture of success in your role

■ the context that you are working in

■ your thinking about the leader you want to be.

Bear these outcomes in mind as you begin to consider your developmental priorities.

There are many ways to action plan. Indeed, you may already be an expert in this area and have a tried and tested method in your toolkit – if so, then plan to use it now.

Here, we offer three tools for you to experiment with if you would like to:

- the Leader iD grid
- the Leader iD priority plan
- the Leader iD reflection sheet.

Below you will find the three tools, a short explanation of how to use them and a real example to guide you.

LEADER iD GRID

The Leader iD grid is a very straightforward five-step approach to helping you use the results from your Leader iD profile and the learning you have taken from reading this book to prioritise where you will focus your efforts. It offers a simple process that leads to focused action.

STEP 1

Bearing in mind …

- the outcomes and reflections from your Leader iD profile
- your ideas from reading the insights
- work done on 'the leader you want to be'
- the demands being made on your role

… which of the 45 insights are you choosing to focus your practice on in the coming weeks and months?

STEP 2

Write these insights into the appropriate column in the following grid along with the strategy the insight relates to and the score you gave yourself for each out of 10.

Leadership insight	Strategy	Ideal level	Leader iD profile level	Review 1	Review 2
		10			
		10			
		10			
		10			
		10			
		10			
		10			
		10			
		10			
		10			

STEP 3

If, like most people, you have identified about 10 insights, you will find this is overwhelming. So it may be better to focus on two or three to start with and return to the others in turn as you make progress.

STEP 4

Below is space to write your three immediate priorities for practice.

From the scores on the grid and my assessment of the context I am working in, the three behaviours I wish to focus on are:

Priority insight 1:

Priority insight 2:

Priority insight 3:

STEP 5

On the grid use the final two columns to re-score yourself on each of the insights at a future date. What progress are you making and how?

Here is an illustration of how to use the grid (for three insights only). You can see that the Leader iD profile identified three areas where practice is required. It shows how much progress was made at two intervals after the respondent has tried the strategies and tips shared in this book.

Leadership insight	Strategy	Ideal level	Leader iD profile level	Review 1 15/06	Review 2 14/10
4. I exercise a sense of duty and social responsibility for the common good of the business.	Compassion	10	5	5	6
32. I illustrate to others how their ambitions can be fulfilled.	Advocates excellence	10	6	7	8
43. I treat people as individuals and coach them towards excellence.	Develops excellence	10	3	4	7

LEADER iD PRIORITY PLAN

The Leader iD priority plan builds on the Leader iD grid. It requires you to take an overview of your areas for development and describe in detail how you are going to make progress. Challenge yourself here to be really specific about the steps you are going to take to get better.

STEP 1

Take the three priorities you have identified from your Leader iD grid and consider the specific activities that you would like to be the focus of your practice. Use the respective insight pages from the book for ideas about how you can fill in the 'Activity' columns that follow.

STEP 2

Complete the columns for each activity including:

■ the frequency of your practice
■ the impact you intend the activity to have on others and your results

- what you will notice as you practise, such as your own and others responses and feelings, as well as outcomes
- the date on which you intend to start practising.

Priority insight 1

Activity	Frequency	What impact do I want to have?	What will I notice?	Start date

Priority insight 2

Activity	Frequency	What impact do I want to have?	What will I notice?	Start date

Priority insight 3

Activity	Frequency	What impact do I want to have?	What will I notice?	Start date

Here is an example of a plan completed for insight 43: I treat people as individuals and coach them towards excellence.

Activity	Frequency	What impact do I want to have?	What will I notice?	Start date
Use more of a coaching style in performance reviews	Monthly reviews	Help others to think for themselves	I will be asking more questions and talking less	June review sessions
Discover hopes, dreams, values and desire of my team	Daily conversations with individuals	Show I am curious, build warmth, create a stronger platform for coaching conversations	I am more able to engage at a human level and make connections about what matters	Daily, starting tomorrow
Help team members to set clear goals	Monthly reviews	Fuel motivation and drive alignment around team goals	Team members are more energised and have a stronger sense of priorities	June review sessions

LEADER iD REFLECTION SHEET

In the early chapters of this book we introduced the relevance of reflection on practice and developing the ability to notice what is happening to you and around you. The best leaders we know are experts at analysing their own performance at work – regularly. They make a habit out of it and regard it as a key discipline on the road to discovering what works for them and what doesn't. Also, importantly, what works or doesn't work in a specific environment or organisational context.

By paying attention to what is happening around you, and the impact you are having, you will navigate your route to your own Leader iD. Making time to reflect on your day's work affords you the opportunity to connect with what is working for you and what isn't so that you can make adjustments in your approach as you go. Learning to step back to witness what is happening and observing yourself in action is key to your development.

Try to complete the following sheet once a day and see what you can discover that will help you be even better tomorrow. When you have completed a few sheets, review them collectively. What do you notice? What are the patterns?

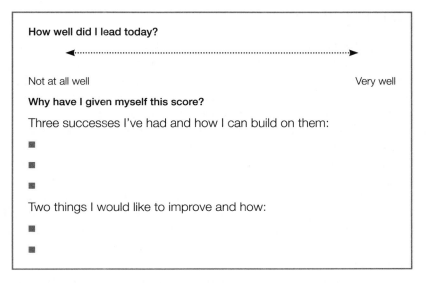

How well did I lead today?

Not at all well   Very well

Why have I given myself this score?

Three successes I've had and how I can build on them:

■

■

■

Two things I would like to improve and how:

■

■

Here is an example of a completed Leader iD reflection sheet.

How well did I lead today?

Not at all well   Very well

Why have I given myself this score?

I attempted to ask more questions and listen better in my review conversations but found myself interrupting people's responses – so good marks for experimenting but could do better with execution...

Three successes I've had and how I can build on them:

■ Much sharper questions – giving me confidence to try more.

■ Really focused on listening well – need to concentrate harder.

■ Showed good interest in people's human side – need to develop confidence to go deeper.

Two things I would like to improve and how:

■ Goal setting is very loose – need to get much sharper and precise. Pay attention to motivational elements for team member.

■ Need to prepare my own mindset prior to reviews so I am not distracted by thinking about other work matters during sessions. Notice my concentration levels mid-session and correct.

FINAL THOUGHTS

Excellent leaders lead for the right reasons. They genuinely care about becoming better people and leaders in order to make a positive impact on the world. People, especially groups of people, need someone to lead, set a direction and be an example to follow. A leader's identity is what determines the direction they set and the example they provide.

There is no shortcut to developing the foundations of good leadership. However, our work and the research that surrounds it tells us that it is not only possible but is essential if we are to prepare organisations for the challenges of the future. Leader iD can be acquired only through consistent practice of the right thoughts and behaviours until they become habitual – until they become part of who you are and how you do things. The case for Leader iD has never been stronger. Leaders influence results by creating healthy work environments that enable people to deliver excellence every day.

As a leader, you drive the character of the business and you must take responsibility for creating the conditions in which learning can take place. This responsibility starts with you being prepared to develop your 'self'.

BIBLIOGRAPHY

Bachkirova, T. (2012) *Developmental Coaching – Developing the Self. The Wiley-Blackwell Handbook of the Psychology of Coaching and Mentoring.*

Bessel van der Kolk, A. (2014) *The Body Keeps the Score: Brain, Mind, and Body in the Healing of Trauma.* New York: Viking.

Bloom, H. K. (2000) *Global brain: The Evolution of Mass Mind from the Big Bang to the 21st Century.* New York: Wiley and Sons.

Chambliss, D. (1989) 'Mundanity of Excellence', *Sociological Theory*, vol. 7, issue 1, pp. 70–86.

De Neve, J.-E., Mikhaylov, S., Dawes, C. T., Christakis, N. A. and Fowler, J. H. (2013) 'Born to lead? A twin design and genetic association study of leadership role occupancy', *The Leadership Quarterly*, 24(1), 45–60.

Drucker, P. via https://www.thepositiveencourager.global/bernard-haldanes-approach-to-doing-positive-work/. [Accessed: 13.06.17.]

Fredrickson, B. (2009) *Positivity.* New York: Crown Publishers.

Grant, A. M. (2014) *Give and Take: A Revolutionary Approach to Success.* London: Weidenfeld & Nicolson.

Greenleaf, R. K., *et al.* (2002) *Servant Leadership: A Journey into the Nature of Legitimate Power and Greatness.* New York: Paulist Press.

Haldane, B. (1996) *Career Satisfaction and Success: A Guide to Job and Personal Freedom.* Indianapolis: JIST Works.

Hernandez, R. (2015) *Here's What Millennials Want From Their Performance Reviews* accessed via https://www.fastcompany.com/3052988/heres-what-millennials-want-from-their-performance-reviews.

Hill, P. and Turiano, N. (2014) 'Purpose in Life as a Predictor of Mortality Across Adulthood', *Psychological Science*, vol. 25, issue 7, pp. 1482–86.

Hughes, L. and Avey J. (2009) 'Transforming with levity: humor, leadership, and follower attitudes', *Leadership & Organization Development Journal*, vol. 30, issue 6, pp. 540–62.

Ibarra, H. (2003) *Working Identity: Unconventional Strategies for Reinventing your Career.* Boston, Mass: Harvard Business School Press.

Immelt, J. (2004) as quoted in *Fast Company*, no. 81 (April 2004): 96.

Jackson, P., Delehanty, H. and Bradley, B. (2014) *Sacred Hoops: Spiritual Lessons as a Hardwood Warrior.* New York, N.Y: Hachette.

Kashdan, T. B. (2010) *Curious? Discover the Missing Ingredient to a Fulfilling Life*. New York: Harper.

Krech, G. (2014) *The Art of Taking Action: Lessons from Japanese Psychology*. Monkton, VT: ToDo Institute.

Kouzes, J. M., and Posner, B. (2017) *The Leadership Challenge: How to Make Extraordinary Things Happen in Organizations*. Hoboken, New Jersey: Leadership Challenge, A Wiley Brand.

Peters, T. J. and Austin, N. (1986) *A Passion for Excellence: The Leadership Difference*. New York, N.Y: Warner Books.

Petrie, N. (2014) *Future Trends in Leadership Development*. Center for Creative Leadership (CCL).

Pundt, A. (2015) 'The relationship between humorous leadership and innovative behavior', *Journal of Managerial Psychology*, vol. 30, issue 8 pp. 878–93.

Roosevelt, E. (2011) You *Learn by Living: Eleven Keys for a More Fulfilling Life*. New York: Harper Perennial.

Senge, P. M. (2006) *The Fifth Discipline: The Art and Practice of the Learning Organization*. New York: Doubleday/Currency.

Sinar, E. *et al*. (2014) 'Ready-Now Leaders: Meeting Tomorrow's Business Challenges', *Global Leadership Forecast,* DDI.

Skills Commission (2014) 'Still in Tune? The Skills System and The Changing Structures of Work' accessed via http://www.policyconnect.org.uk/sc/sites/site_sc/files/report/429/fieldreportdownload/stillintunetheskillssystemandthechangingstructuresofwork.pdf.

TalentSmoothie (2017) 'Employee Value Proposition Factsheet' accessed via https://talentsmoothie.com/ts1/wp-content/uploads/2017/05/employee-value-proposition-evp-factsheet-talentsmoothie-v2.pdf.

van Vugt, M. and Ronay, R. (2014) 'The evolutionary psychology of leadership: Theory, review, and roadmap', *Organizational Psychology Review*, 4(1), 74–95.

Vijay, S. and Singh, H. (2015) *Global Human Capital Trends*. Deloitte University Press.

Wallis, G. P. and Pilbeam, D. (2016) *How to Become a Talented Performer: A Formula for Early Career Success*. FastPrint Publishing, Peterborough, England.

Wiseman, L. (2017) *Multipliers: How the Best Leaders Make Everyone Smarter*. New York, NY: HarperBusiness, an imprint of HarperCollins Publishers.

Wooden, J. and Carty, J. (2015) *Coach Wooden's Pyramid of Success*. Grand Rapids, Michigan: Revell, a division of Baker Publishing Group.

Woodward, C. (2005) *Winning*. London: Hodder.

INDEX